Norman

Once I was the Dean of King's
Now I am the King of Deans.

Robert

June, 1996

ERIC MILNER MILNER-WHITE

Eric Milner-White, Dean of York. (Photograph: The Dean and Chapter of York.)

ERIC MILNER MILNER-WHITE

C.B.E., D.S.O., M.A., D.D., Litt.D.,
Dean of York 1941–1963

A MEMORIAL
edited by
Robert Tinsley Holtby
M.A., B.D., F.S.A.,
Dean of Chichester 1977–1989

Beauty in all its forms speaks an eternal voice

Published by PHILLIMORE on behalf of
THE FRIENDS OF YORK MINSTER

1991

Published by
PHILLIMORE & CO. LTD.
Shopwyke Hall, Chichester, Sussex

ISBN 0 85033 813 1

*Publication of this Memorial
has been made possible through
the kind generosity of*
THE FRIENDS OF YORK MINSTER
Church House,
Ogleforth, York, YO1 2JN

Phototypeset by Intype, London
Printed by Chichester Press Limited

Contents

List of Plates

Preface

The following essays mark the fiftieth anniversary (27 October 1991) of the installation of Eric Milner Milner-White as Dean of York.

Two memoirs, published shortly after the Dean's death in 1963,[1] record biographical matter which is not in detail repeated here, where the main (though not exclusive) emphasis rests on the York period.

The essays are a critical tribute to a remarkable occupant of the Deanery of York, who in several respects was unsurpassed in the long history of the Cathedral and Metropolitical Church of St. Peter. A discriminatory estimate should not diminish the acknowledged stature of a notable personality, man and priest.

The *ad hoc* committee which designed this volume considered that certain aspects of the Dean's activity and interests deserved particular attention, and we are grateful to the authors who describe them. In the general essay the *facts* are based on documents: the *judgements* are the sole responsibility of the writer. Throughout, the Dean is referred to as 'Milner', the designation by which he was customarily known, though, both in correspondence and direct address, formality was preserved. The usage implies no claim to familiarity.

A list of acknowledgements is appended. Here warm gratitude is recorded to the Friends of York Minster, who promoted this memorial volume, and to their Secretary, Mr. James Fairbairn, ever kind and helpful.

Robert Holtby

October, 1991.

---

1. Patrick Wilkinson, *Eric Milner-White, 1884–1963 . . . a Memoir*, (King's College, Cambridge, 1963); Philip Pare and Donald Harris, *Eric Milner-White, 1884–1963: a Memoir*, (S.P.C.K., 1965).

Foreword

His Royal Highness the Duke of Kent, K.G.

Eric Milner-White was one of a group of distinguished men who in the 1940s and 50s enriched the life of the Minster and, through that, the city of York.

He will be remembered for his close involvement after the war with putting back the stained glass which had been stored away for safety, and for his extensive additions to the furnishing including the nave pulpit and throne. These now stand testimony to his taste and to the intensity of his interest in the Minster.

As a distinguished academic with a brilliant command of our language Dean Milner-White enriched the English liturgy with memorable prayers and arrangements to services such as the Nine Lesson Christmas Service.

Those who knew him will remember his meticulous care for Minster worship and his close interest in its music. He was a founder of the York Civic Trust and a moving spirit in the establishment of the University. An authority on architecture and glass, he also left an important collection of pottery to York Art Gallery.

But his chief and over-riding concern was for the great Minster of whose Deanery he was one of the most distinguished occupants.

Acknowledgements

Gratitude is chiefly owed to Mr. Bernard Barr, F.S.A., and the staff of York Minster Library for their unfailing help, courtesy and patience; and to Mrs. Marie Carrington for her efficient secretarial work. The Dean and Chapter of York are thanked for permission to use the Milner-White papers. We are also grateful to the following for invaluable help:

The Borthwick Institute of Historical Research
The Reverend Dr. Owen Chadwick, O.M., K.B.E., F.B.A.
The Right Reverend Lord Coggan, P.C.
Miss Jacqueline Cox
Mr. Michael Dryland
Mrs. (Lalage) Fair (née Milner-White)
Canon Donald Gray, T.D.
Miss Marjory Green
Mr. Richard Green
Mr. Kenneth Harrison, F.S.A.
The Reverend Jeremy Haselock
Mr. Robert Henderson
Mr. A. T. Howat
Dr. Francis Jackson, O.B.E.
Lord James of Rusholme
Mr. Ralph Keeping
The Right Reverend Eric Kemp
The Reverend Noel Kemp-Welch
King's College, Cambridge, The Provost and Scholars
Canon Philip Lamb
Mr. C. B. McCarter
The Reverend John McMullen
Canon P. C. Magee
Mr. John Mitchell
St. Peter's School, York, the Headmaster
Miss Helena Randall
Mr. George Rylands, C.H., C.B.E.
Dr. John Shannon, O.B.E.
Miss Barbara Snape
The Very Reverend Henry Stapleton, F.S.A.
Canon Christopher Stead, F.B.A.
Canon David Stewart-Smith
Mrs. (Kathleen) Stewart-Smith
Miss Pauline Vanes
Mr. Irvine Watson, O.B.E.
Dr. Hilary Wayment, O.B.E., F.S.A.
The late Mr. John West-Taylor, O.B.E.
Sir Marcus Worsley, Bart., F.S.A.
York City Art Gallery

Eric Milner-White

Robert Holtby

Eric Milner Milner-White was installed as Dean of York on 27 October 1941, the eve of the Feast of St Simon and St Jude. Born on St George's Day (23 April) 1884, he was therefore 57 on his appointment. He died on 15 June 1963.

His 22 years of office began in the dark days of war. Less than a year after his arrival, on 29 April 1942, the 'Baedeker' air-raid on York caused serious damage, including the destruction of the Guildhall and St Martin's church. The Minster was untouched in that and other raids, but it clearly lacked the meticulous care possible in peacetime. The glass had been removed, and the restoration of the North Transept roof had been temporarily abandoned.

At the end of the war the City itself faced problems, not only of physical restoration, but of policy: '. . . conflict between two possible future rôles for York: as a primarily business, shopping and administrative centre for a wide region, welcoming population and traffic growth, or as a modest-sized historic city increasingly dependent on cultural and tourist interests'.[1]

The answer to these questions had major consequences for planning and architectural development and, above all, for strategy on conservation. The City was particularly fortunate at that time to benefit from the idealism and practical acumen of Alderman J. B. Morrell, who in 1940 had published his vision of what York, replanned, could be.[2]

The new Dean wasted no time in beginning the enrichment of the furnishings of the Minster, but from 1945 his activity in and for the City assumed increasing influence, and his friendship with Morrell was the key factor in facilitating it.

But who was this divine of whom very few York citizens had heard? He had spent most of his life within the confines of King's College, Cambridge, where as an undergraduate, from Harrow School, he had achieved considerable academic distinction in history. After study at Cuddesdon Theological College and two short curacies, he had become Chaplain of King's and a Lecturer in History at Corpus Christi College. From 1918 he was a Fellow and Dean of King's, and remained there until the move to York (the offer of the Deanery of Salisbury having been declined). Widely travelled, he was renowned in ecclesiastical and

---

1. John Hutchinson and D. M. Palliser, *York*, 1980, p. 84 (Bartholomew City Guides).
2. The City of our Dreams.

Plate 1. Eric Milner-White, *c.*1912. (Photograph reproduced by permission of The Provost and Scholars of King's College, Cambridge.)

academic circles for his many-sided knowledge of the arts and crafts, glass especially and architecture, for his devotion to the ballet and for his authorship of prayers. Few of the many who heard on the wireless the Festival of Nine Lessons, with Carols, from King's on Christmas Eve would know that the Dean of York had 'ordered' that service in its well-known form (the Dean of King's was not one of the designated nine readers). To the perceptive among the citizens of York and to Church people in the Diocese the appointment might well have appeared providential, given the tasks to be faced and the distinctive qualities of the Crown's nominee.

But one chapter in Milner's career presented a sharp contrast to his many years in Cambridge. He had been mentioned in despatches, and in 1918 awarded the D.S.O. for bravery while serving on the Western front in the Great War (for some time he was also in Italy). Volunteering as a Chaplain in 1914, he served with the Seventh Division of the British Expeditionary Force, becoming Senior Chaplain in 1917. His personal courage in battle was outstanding, and at one critical moment, when officers had been killed, he assumed command (contrary to convention in the Chaplains' Department). Certainly he earned the displeasure of Bishop Taylor-Smith, the Chaplain-General, whose strongly Evangelical views were affronted by the theological outlook of some of the (non-regular) chaplains. In a volume entitled *The Church in the Furnace*[1] Milner wrote on 'Worship and Services', lamenting not only the widespread ignorance of the troops in matters of faith, but also the inadequacy of the services of the Prayer Book (particularly the office for the burial of the dead) to meet the desperate conditions of trench warfare. The Prayer Book, he affirmed, helped only the instructed: 'We never guessed of old how removed it was from common wants; nor how intellectual are its prayers and forms of devotion.'.[2]

The distinguished war record and radical criticism of the chaplaincy establishment were unsuspected by those who first set eyes on the new Dean – shy in manner, reserved, somewhat precious in speech, a King's don. The next 22 years were to reveal a combination of creative imagination and resolute will, to the benefit alike of Minster and City.

Neither the building nor the local community, however, had the first call on Milner's ministry in York, dedicated though he was to the services of both. It was the daily round of worship – as at King's – which was his great joy, as it was his first duty. The *opus Dei*, the offices and the Eucharist, he believed to be the foundation of his work – belief resting on deep conviction, not mere statutory obligation. His faithfulness in these observances must be remembered even when the account which follows recalls elements of human fallibility. Devotion *in* the Minster was the foundation for devotion *to* it.

The scope of Milner's initiatives is to be seen most tellingly in the Annual Reports of the Friends of York Minster, which constitute a

1. ed. F. B. Macnutt, 1917.
2. *op. cit.*, p. 184.

record of considerable historical importance. They tell not only of the acquisition of ornaments and furnishings, of restoration and adornment, but recount also year by year much of Minster life and the doings of its clergy and officers. Each Report had a separate account of those activities for which the Clerk of Works was responsible and (after the War) a progress report on the replacement of the glass.

The key 'text' for Milner was his declaration of intent in the 1942 Report: 'We shall be united in the passion to make the Minster still more glorious within'.[1] In that same year the Report, his first, had an article on the ironwork – a pointer to his detailed command of skilled craftsmanship.

Si monumentum requiris . . . The visitor to the Minster sees all around him the evidence of work promoted by Milner: textiles (described elsewhere in this volume), new stalls in the Nave (the gift of Lady Milner-White), Robert Thompson's stalls in the Lady Chapel, the font cover by Sir Ninian Comper (1944 – an early commission), the Nave pulpit, also by Comper, memorial to Archbishops Lang and Temple, and the Archbishop's throne in the Nave, memorial to Archbishop Garbett, designed by Sir Albert Richardson. Milner was especially proud of the Astronomical Clock, a memorial to the Allied Air Forces, also designed by Richardson. When the Gospel ambo was installed in the Choir, a memorial to Sqn. Leader Kenneth Thomas Peart Terry D.F.C., Milner reproduced in the 1953 Report an illustration of the ambo at Torcello, an impressive precedent.

There were smaller additions over which equal care (the *mot juste*) was taken: Lady de Grimston's refreshing of the decoration on memorials, gold leaf on the stalls in the Choir, vestments, a new lectern Bible, altar ornaments, and much more, to enrich yet further the treasures of the Minster, all recorded in the Annual Reports.

Of the Nave fittings – Pulpit (1948), Choir stalls (1948), Dean's and Canons' stalls (1952) and Throne (1959) – it has been observed that they were 'intended for traditional ceremonial, unconformable to fancy liturgical layout'.[2] Without commenting on a later reordering of the Nave sanctuary, it has to be acknowledged that Milner's scheme indeed presupposed 'traditional ceremonial'.

Reading the Annual Reports provokes the question: how were these admirable undertakings paid for? Milner's personal generosity played its part: the encouraging of donors was persuasively pursued, and visits to London proved fruitful. An account in the 1949 Report described a visit to the Antique Dealers' Fair: 'In the first booth I entered, behold what would remove our reproach – a rare musical desk of Jacobean date (say 1620), characteristically carven, remarkably constructed, out of one piece of elm'.[3] (The 'reproach' was the desk for the Master of the Music, inferior in design.) A Mrs. Bellis of Bournemouth 'saw me thus captivated, and heard my proposal', and offered to pay. A native

1. 1940 *Report*, p. 3.
2. Hutchinson and Pallister, *op. cit.*, p. 116.
3. 1949 *Report*, p. 13

of Yorkshire, she was proud to offer a gift for the Minster, and the Report continued: 'protests moved neither Mrs. Bellis nor her husband then or thereafter; and the fruit of their generous insistence all can now see between the Choir-stalls'.[1] (A platform for the desk had been designed by Richardson.) It would strain credulity somewhat to suppose that protest was very emphatic. It was a great tribute to the respect for Milner's artistic discrimination that Friends often learned, apparently without demur, that they were expected to pay for acquisitions resulting from his indefatigable searches.

The Reports gave some attention to the Minster fabric. The completion of the work on the North Transept roof was noted in the 1951 Report. In 1950 there was the serious business of the repairs to the west front. Hence an appeal – 'we won't quail'[2] – for £250,000 of which £50,000 was still lacking when the 1959 Report was made, when also prices were rising and the organ needed restoration. In 1958 two south Nave buttresses had moved out of perpendicular, with a consequent crack. 'This Dean hates begging',[3] said of gifts for interior furnishings, was certainly applicable to fabric restoration.

The Precincts drew an occasional reference – Dean's Park, St William's College Green – and great services in the Minster earned special comment, enthronement of Archbishops (Garbett, Ramsey, Coggan), royal visits, and, very prominently, the marriage of the Duke and Duchess of Kent.[4] Milner welcomed the televising of that notable event, but had been worried about the inconvenience to the Minster entailed in preparation for television broadcasts of regular services. An Easter T.V. transmission had involved 13 weeks' preparation.[5]

For the chronicler who seeks to penetrate the daily life of the Minster in Milner's time, the record of appointments (and departures) of staff, clerical and lay, is illuminating. That record also illustrates the very personal character of Milner's preference in the choice of officers. Many such were admirable, and fulfilled expectations, particularly in their rôle in the offering of the worship. The songmen were extolled on retirement for their service to the Minster (referred to by their surnames only); for the work on the glass the 'masterly combination of Lazenby and Gibson' was noted, as Milner looked back shortly before his death.[6] The appointment and departure of vicars-choral were recorded, and the engagement of the Reverend John McMullen to Peggy Keith, Milner's housekeeper, was reported as 'Romance in a Deanery'.[7] Sir Edward Bairstow's death evoked a reflection on the 'reverence and love' which had marked their relationship, and the appointment of Francis Jackson as his successor was announced with enthusiasm.[8]

A well deserved tribute was paid to George Arthur Scaife who was taken ill in 1951. He had become Head Master in 1903 when the Minster Choir School was re-established, and, wrote Milner, 'he did the deed grandly'.[9] His successor, the Reverend D. V. Hewitt, was

1. 1949 *Report*, p. 13. 2. 1950 *Report*, p. 5; 3. 1950 *Report*, p. 6; 4. 1962 *Report*, pp. 1–2; 5. *ibid.*, p. 5, and 1957 *Report* on Christmas,1956, T.V. broadcast, the first T.V. broadcast; 6. 1962 *Report*, p. 9; 7. 1952 *Report*, p. 19; 8. 1946 *Report*, pp. 21–22, and 1947 *Report*, p. 14; 9. 1951 *Report*, p. 7.

appointed with warm commendation, and the second teacher at the Choir School, Miss E. B. Whyte, was described as 'the finest "right-hand" any school could boast'.[1]

A development of considerable consequence was the scheme for honorary chaplains[2] (of the first generation of whom the present writer was one), the intention being to offer to visitors to the Minster spiritual counsel and instruction in the Faith. These were days before the arrival of vast crowds of tourists, but it was an imaginative move, a discreet form of evangelism. In the first World War Milner had been deeply touched by the large numbers who lacked even elementary knowledge of Christianity, yet in the 1950 Report he expressed astonishment that the people of York did not come more to the Minster.[3] He seemed unconscious that, to many, the ecclesiastical (and even social) ambience of the place might appear foreign, even daunting. However, he achieved in great measure the practical fulfilment of his own ideal, however distant it was from the perceptions of the 'ordinary' people of York, and the Reports record that ideal: 'A metropolitical cathedral can look at nothing which is not of the finest'.[4] In his last Report, shortly before his death, he penned his farewell:

'Let me say with all the strength still at my command, how much I have loved the Minster over these twenty one years, how much I have loved the City which it surmounts and crowns, and how grateful I am to the Friends, who with boundless enthusiasm and generosity have worked to make the Minster within as glorious as the Minster without. Ever yours with deep affection and thanks'.[5]

At York Milner will ever be remembered for his major work on the Minster glass, rescued from war-time storage. That work is described elsewhere, and it is beyond doubt that the selection of Mr. Peter Gibson by Milner was remarkably perceptive. Here it is worthwhile noting the existence of a pamphlet, How to choose Stained Glass, sub-titled 'Advice on planning and commissioning a design'.[6] It concerns principally the parish church, though it has obvious relevance to the insertion in the Minster of glass from other places. He insisted that, above all, the glass must be subject to the architecture of a building, drawing attention to 'terrible failures'[7] in thinking of glass as picture-making, partly because stained glass is essentially a mosaic art, and also because the lead cames which hold the glass together form part of the design. Glass is 'an architectural decoration, not a realistic scene or picture in its own right'.[8] Mediaeval glass, he affirmed, very properly lacked perspective, recession, violent movement: some subjects 'dear to piety' were not always appropriate for glass, though the portrayal of the reigning Christ was highly commended: 'That gave the priest, the artist and his material what each wanted – a central doctrinal theme which could be treated with decorative majesty'.[9] He made other points to

1. 1952 Report, p. 17; 2. 1947 Report, p. 4, and 1948 Report, p. 6; 3. p. 4. 4.45 p.m. a 'daily oasis of rest and refreshment'; 4. 1962 Report, p. 11; 5. 1963 Report, p. 14; 6. Undated, but published for the Central Council for the Care of Churches in 1959; 7. ibid., p. 2; 8. ibid., p. 3; 9. p. 5.

which he gave practical expression in his recommendations to the Diocesan Advisory Committee.

The seminal background of this work on the York glass was, of course, his deep knowledge of the glorious glass in King's Chapel. In 1930 Milner wrote an appendix to a reissue of the *Guide to the Windows* by Montague Rhodes James, the authoritative work on that subject. He noted that, since 1899 when the *Guide* was first written, there were three important developments to record: the restoration of 14 windows (including the East Window), under the direction of James himself and by C. E. Kempe (whose work Milner greatly admired); secondly, acceptance of the theory that Dierick Vellert, master glass-painter of Antwerp, had drawn the cartoons for some of the windows;[1] thirdly, the painted glass in the 'side chapels' (18 of them) had been increased (1920–30) by a remarkable series of gifts, and by arrangement there of fragments which Dr. James had removed. Hence the appendix on the side chapel glass was re-written.

Milner did not reveal that this work – and much of the finance involved – was largely his own. Dr. Hilary Wayment dedicated his distinguished work on the Side-Chapel Glass at King's[2] to the memory of Milner, his godfather, noting particularly his special interest in stained and painted quarries. Dr. Wayment concluded: '. . . his embellishment of the side-chapels during the twenties had been an indispensable preparation for the immense task he was to tackle, after the war of 1939–45, at York'.[3]

Milner in the Friends' Annual Reports described the gradual replacement of the Minster glass. Not long before his death he announced at the Regular Chapter (10 July 1962) that the glass of the Chapter House had been put back, 'though in a somewhat different order'.[4] Whatever criticism his work at York attracted, there can be no doubt of his magisterial command of the history of glass, and of the techniques involved in its conservation.

Yet in an objective account of Milner's work something must be said of that adverse criticism which aspects of his reordering of the glass have attracted. That there has been unfavourable comment is here simply recorded as a fact, the writer having no professional competence in this field to express an informed judgement on the issues involved.

The critical view is stated very clearly in the official *History of York Minster*.[5] David E. O'Connor and Jeremy Haselock in the chapter 'Stained and Painted Glass' write as follows:

(Following the appearance of a German Zeppelin in 1916) 'a plan to remove the windows was put into action. This drew attention to the decayed state of much of the glass, and an appeal was launched for a large programme of restoration. The Society for the Protection of Ancient Buildings advised on how this should be conducted. The distinguished committee, reporting on the work, could not "suggest any improvement on the method adopted at York, namely to re-lead the glass in the exact arrangement

1. Dr. N. Beets in the *Burlington Magazine*, LV, October 1907.
2. Cambridge, 1988.
3. *op. cit.*, p. 15.
4. M-W papers, I, 4.
5. Edited by G. E. Aylmer and R. Cant, Oxford, 1977.

in which it is found, and where pieces are actually missing, to fill the holes with plain glass.''

When war struck again in 1939, the enormous task of removing the windows had to commence afresh. Another opportunity for major restoration presented itself. It was carried out by the Minster glaziers under the guidance of the dean, Eric Milner-White. The strictly preservationist approach of the 1920's was abandoned for an attempt to improve the panels by reconstructing them into something approaching their original design. Occasional misreading of their subject-matter has led to iconographic problems. This is further hampered by the lack of full documentation of alterations.'[1]

That was the general criticism of Milner's approach to restoration. It was shared by others, including the late Peter Newton, to whom the two authors express their indebtedness.[2] They acknowledge in a foot-note that there were 'short accounts' each year in the Friends Annual Reports[3] (some of these Reports are indeed short: others give consider-able detail). While they are a valuable record, they do not constitute 'full documentation', but the words of the reports were supplemented by several thousand (black and white) photographs of the panels before and after restoration taken by the then Clerk of Works, and much used by later students of the glass.

Among critics there appears to be unstinted admiration for the resto-ration of the Great East Window. Indeed, O'Connor and Haselock remark that 'The last restoration of the window took place between 1942 and 1952 when mistakes in earlier restoration were corrected and alien intrusions removed.'[4] There is commendation of the re-ordering of panels in the St William window[5] as also of 'skilled restoration' of windows in the North Choir aisle.[6] While examples are given of correct identification,[7] the authors dispute Milner's conclusions in other cases,[8] and criticise him severely in the case of a distinguished corpus of panels, a 'stylistically and iconographically homogeneous group . . . split up and inserted into five windows,' in which groups are included two further panels in the Nave,[9] all of 'superb quality of design and execution.' One other critic asks if Milner really understood the distinc-tion of these panels.[10]

Milner's conclusions in his pamphlet, *Sixteenth Century Glass in York Minster and in the Church of St Michael-le-Belfrey*, published in 1960,[11] have been widely criticised. But the most damaging charge is made by O'Connor and Haselock. 'In 1845,' they write, 'a legacy made money available for a restoration which had disastrous results for the east window (of the Chapter House). This in turn fell victim to another restorer under whose direction the glass was removed in 1959 to make way for the present motley collection. This decision destroyed at a stroke both the iconographic integrity and the aesthetic harmony of the building which the Victorian restorers had at least preserved . . . It is difficult to ascertain from the confused and mutilated state of some one hundred and forty narrative panels, whether the consistent plan,

1.   O'Connor and Haselock in Aylmer and Cant, *op. cit.*, p. 316;   2.   *ibid.* p. 393, note;   3.   *ibid.*, p. 316, n. 8;   4.   *ibid.*, p. 364;   5.   *ibid.*, p. 377 (surveyed by J. Fowler, *Yorkshire Arch. and Top. Journal*, vol. 3, 1873–4);   6.   *ibid.*, p. 374;   7.   e.g. p. 358, n. 189;   8.   e.g. panels in the South Transept, p. 345, and the 'Pilgrimage' window, p. 354, n. 180;   9.   *ibid.*, p. 378;   10.   In a letter to the author (others have made this point);   11.   St Anthony's Hall Publications, No. 17, 1960 (and described in the Friends *Annual Report* for 1959, pp. 28–37).

which is such a feature of the design of the glass, extends to the iconographic scheme'.[1] Further, the authors claim that the skilled work of restoration by John Barnett in the middle of the 19th century, approved in 1845 by the *Ecclesiologist*, did not please Dean Milner-White, 'who removed the figure panels after the war to make room for medieval glass from other parts of the Minster.'[2]

What is the non-specialist observer to conclude? The extracts from the official history of the Minster, together with other critical comments, point to mistakes. That can hardly be questioned. In theory Milner could perhaps have consulted more widely, though this possibility in the given circumstances had its difficulties. Certainly, jumbles needed restoring to order – even an amateur observer would expect this, and would suppose that judgement would not be infallible. Aged 57 on appointment (with four years of war still to go) Milner was anxious to complete a restoration which he judged would take twenty years. (The Chapter House work was finished shortly before his death, when he was already suffering from the illness which was to prove terminal.) Moreover, the restoration of the glass, absorbing though it was, had to be undertaken in the midst of many other (major) activities in Minster and City.

There is widespread agreement that the restoration of the Great East Window was a triumph and an unqualified approbation for skilled restoration elsewhere. What strikes the 'outside' observer is the immensity of the task in York Minster. Angels themselves would blanch at the prospect of undertaking it. Certainly no cathedral dignitary at that time could equal Milner in his command of the history and iconography of glass.

It was Milner's very cast of mind and imagination which seem on occasion to have led him astray. The same distinctive qualities made for his remarkable achievement.

Care for the standard of the music was one of Milner's chief preoccupations. Music is the handmaid of worship, and cathedrals are traditionally committed to musical excellence. By no one was this regard for musical standards more intensely felt than the Dean of York. At King's he was, of course, well versed in Church music, and had worked happily with two successive Organists, 'Daddy' Mann and Bernhard (Boris) Ord, the latter Organist from 1929. On Boris's appointment the character of the Chapel bills began to change, 'far more sixteenth century music being included, and in matters of musical taste there was a firm bond between Boris and Milner-White'.[3] The pointing of the Psalms was altered, moving one conservatively inclined chorister to write home with the comment, 'That loony Ord has been messing the Psalms about'.[4]

At York, Sir Edward Bairstow was the Organist (from 1913), a very different character from Ord, though both were given to plain speech.

1. *op. cit.*, pp. 334–5 and 339.
2. *ibid.*, p. 392.
3. Philip Radcliffe, *Bernhard (Boris) Ord*, 1962, p. 10, Henry Arthur Mann, 1850–1929.
4. *ibid.*

Boris and Milner as Fellows of the College were equal in status: Bairstow, however eminent, was a servant of the Dean and Chapter. In Dean Bate's time there had been some differences, but the Milner-Bairstow relationship was good, achieving its most notable expression in the 'Lamentation', where words from Jeremiah selected by Milner were matched by 'the perfection of beauty' in Bairstow's music: a partnership of inspiration.

However, it was not long before Bairstow's health declined, and he died in May, 1946. Francis Jackson, an ex-chorister, had already been appointed Assistant Organist, though in the event on leaving the Army he became effectively acting-Organist, as Bairstow was ill. Five months after the latter's death, on 8 October the Regular Chapter appointed Francis Jackson to succeed him. It was Milner's choice, though Jackson was as well known to the Precentor (Charles Bell) and to the Chancellor (Frederick Harrison). Given the subsequent reputation of Jackson as executant and composer, it is clear that the appointment was both imaginative, and justified on the grounds of a record already proven. (Jackson was 29, ten years older than James Nares, who was 19 when he was appointed in 1734.)

Milner with his wide knowledge of and sensitivity to Church music introduced changes for which he argued persuasively. A weekly meeting with the Organist and the Sub-Chanter determined the music for the following week, and the widening of the repertoire which had begun in Bairstow's time was further increased. Milner was very fond of Charles Wood, whom he had known in Cambridge, and whose works he commended. Kenneth Leighton's *Magnificat* he thought was 'like a tragic ballet'. Some Latin anthems were approved, but English settings only were allowed for the normal Sunday Sung Eucharist and for the canticles. Tudor Church Music editions were encouraged, presumably based on experience at King's. A change in the Psalter from the Bairstow, Buck, Macpherson pointing to *The Psalter Newly Pointed* offended Chancellor Harrison (when he heard of it!) with his ingrained sense of the superiority of Bairstow.

Although Milner maintained a tight and detailed control over the repertoire, the weekly meeting was a useful forum for discussion, which inevitably also offered the opportunity for comment on other matters.

It was a difficult time for recruiting songmen, though the number was raised to ten. Milner was always worried about finance, and hence resisted the raising of salaries. (One songman was informed in 1950 that he was granted a pension of £1 a week!) He courteously thanked the choir, but seemed to act on the premise that the privilege of sharing actively in the worship was the reward beside which no other could be deemed worthy of very serious consideration.

Decanal efforts to assume the rôle of Precentor were not successful:

intoning the office did not rise to the standard set by its practitioner in all other areas of worship, and that truth seems to have dawned on Milner.

'Beauty in all its forms speaks an eternal voice'.[1] Such was his general conviction, but it was said of the beauty of music.

Mr. Bernard Barr has described the history of the Minster Library, and paid tribute to the unequalled 'zest, vision and practicality'[2] shown by Milner in connection with its 'little renaissance'.

A report on the Library in 1933 by H. R. Creswick for various reasons failed to be implemented, and nothing came of a proposal two years later to erect an archive building. There was a decline in the running of the Library, though a service was maintained through the devoted work of Canon Frederick Harrison (former Vicar-Choral, then Chancellor, and Librarian from 1925) and an Assistant, Miss Elizabeth Brunskill, to whom the Library owed much over a period of more than twenty-five years.

Even in the War years there were signs of a new beginning – acquisitions[3] and new shelving – and in 1945 the Special Fabric Restoration Fund was converted into the Minster Library Fund. This was an irony of history. Two Caxtons and other books had been sold in 1930 for £20,000, as Sir Walter Tapper (the Minster Consultant Architect) had recommended urgent repairs, the estimated cost of which could not in the then Dean's view be raised wholly by appeal. The residue thus came back to the Library, the work on the fabric in the event having been scaled down.

This was not the sole source of finance over the next few years: Milner was himself a generous donor; Pilgrim Trust grants were secured; the Treasurer, Canon Addleshaw, enthusiastic for the welfare of the Library, diverted funds for its use. Six handsome bookcases were added in 1946.

Harrison resigned in 1956, and died shortly afterwards. The second stage of the Library development began with the appointment of Canon Reginald Cant as Chancellor and the Report on the Library by A. N. L. Munby, Librarian of King's (well known, of course, to Milner). The policy emerging from that Report was that the inherited collections should be conserved and made available; that the modern collection should be extended and used for academic research in York; thirdly, that there should be provision for theological reading by the clergy. A key document is the paper on the Library written by Canon Cant in the Friends Report of June 1957. In 1959–60 an extension was added to house muniments (until then in the Zouche Chapel) and the Hailstone Collection of Yorkshire local history. This was financed by the Dean, whose other gifts were often bestowed under the disguise 'Philologus'. A further extension for a Reading Room, also partly paid for by Milner, followed in 1963, and almost all his books passed to the Library on his

1. M-W Papers II.8, 24 November, 1953.
2. Aylmer and Cant, op. cit., p. 532 (C. B. L. Barr).
3. Particularly notable 'A Mediaeval "Hours" of the York Use' (Friends Report, 1944, pp. 14–18).

death. The appointment of a professional staff in 1961 led in 1964 to the taking over by the University of part of the full-time staffing of the Library.[1] The only failure was the scheme for the establishment of 'Friends of the Minster Library' which in the event fell far below Milner's expectations.[2]

That York Minster Library is foremost among Cathedral libraries, and highly regarded in academic circles, is due primarily to the quality of its staff, as well as the equally high quality and variety of its contents. But achievement would not have been possible without that characteristic blend of vision and practicality – idealism and realism – which marked Milner's undertakings. This was a great work for York, for the Minster, and for scholarship.

A cathedral is the principal church of the diocese and its dean the chief presbyter. His duties are exercised primarily in the cathedral, but each dean has to ask himself how best he can serve the Christian community in his area. It was the Chairmanship of the Diocesan Advisory Committee which provided for Milner an influential rôle. His extensive knowledge and distinctive skills were exercised in a wide variety of recommendations on the furnishings of churches. In October 1944, he succeeded the Archdeacon of York, A. C. England, and was actively engaged in the work, save when ill, until January 1963. The Committee minutes,[3] now housed in the Borthwick Institute, record faithful attendance and close attention to detail. They also witness to visits paid to churches, without which distant discussion, occasionally unavoidable, lacked some degree of reality. Meetings were usually held at the Deanery, though from 1946 to 1950 in 4, Minster Yard.

The impression made by the record is that of a strong Chairman whose opinions and artistic judgements were never less than definite. He had set out his basic principles, together with some practical counsel, in an address, 'Goodness, Truth and Beauty' given to the chairmen and secretaries of D.A.C.s at their conference in Cambridge in April 1956 (published in *Your Parish Church*, the twelfth Report of the Central Council for the Care of Churches).[4] That God was Beauty as well as Truth was the axiom of his argument, and his text came from Irenaeus, 'The Vision of God is the Life of Man'. He saw beauty in churches as a manifestation of the work of the Spirit, and as a reflection of the New Jerusalem, of which 'servitors we now are here within its actual walls'.[5] 'It has always been a motto of mine that every single church in this land can be made a shrine'.[6]

From these high principles, his genuine inspiration, he moved to practical advice under the heading 'Towards Perfection': cleanliness in churches, order and neatness ('Order is the grace which makes for restfulness')[7] and SPACE – 'room for God to breathe.' In this address he contended that architecture was the 'mistress art', recalling his

1. M-W Papers VI.1, 10 Feb., 1962, gives details on proposals for links with the University.
2. Friends *Report*, 1944, pp. 19–22, a statement by Milner on the Library.
3. D. A. C. ref. MB 5, 6, 7;   4. 1957;   5. *ibid.*, p. 3;   6. p. 3;   7. p. 3.

reminder elsewhere that all furnishing, all art, must be fashioned to accord with its architectural context. Above all, worship was the heart of beauty.

He urged lengthier meetings, visits to churches, 'one or two joint picnics,' to increase 'the unity and zest and merriment of our committee's fellowship'.[1] Evidently there had been such picnics in the Diocese of Ely, where he had been a member of the D.A.C.

Milner had a good committee, which included Canon J. S. Purvis and Professor Hamilton Thompson (an infrequent attender): W. J. Green, the Minster Clerk of Works, was also a member. Two successive Secretaries were priests from the Minster: D. C. Stewart-Smith (King's and Cuddesdon), Vicar-Choral, Sacrist, and (later) Sub-Chanter; from 1949 A. J. McMullen (King's and Cuddesdon), Vicar-Choral, Sub-Chanter and Sacrist, and the third, from 1959, was H. E. C. Stapleton, then Curate of Pocklington (now Dean of Carlisle). The bland minutes convey but a faint impression of the reality of the discussions among members of a powerful committee led by a determined Chairman. They reveal, however, Milner's known personal choices in the commissioning of work – notably George Pace, the architect, and Thompson of Kilburn for woodwork. In December 1958, the Committee had to express a view on Epstein's 'Ecce Homo', proposed for Selby Abbey. Pace was the architect employed by the Abbey, and was much in favour of the work. Following some discussion on the question of *site*, the Committee decided (9 votes for, one abstention) to recommend in favour, and the Central Council for the Care of Churches was asked to consider the project in the light of the D.A.C.'s favourable conclusion.[2]

Matters of general principles were never forgotten. Thus at Nunthorpe, over a proposal for a window by Hugh Easton (18 July 1949), Milner, unavoidably absent, sent a note: 'We cannot but pass this window on the score of decorative design and drawing. But we would remit to the Chancellor's discretion and determination two further problems it suggests.

1. To what extent are designs with such *personal* reference desirable in a parish church?
2. How far may Scriptural words and incidents be applied to a purpose far removed from their context?'[3]

The Diocesan Advisory Committee, it may assuredly be claimed, enjoyed in its Chairman a priest of passionate commitment to the care and beauty of churches. A report on a visit to North Grimston, the placing of a picture in Hackness, discussion on gates at Grosmont, exemplified, in the early stages of his tenure of the office,[4] Milner's unfailing attention to detail in pursuance of his declared maxim that every church should be a shrine.

1. p. 4.
2. MB6, 1 December, 1958.
3. MB5, 18 July, 1949.
4. MB5.

Milner's still wider influence on the Church was exercised in the Province through his (ex officio) membership of the Northern Convocation. His regular speeches there – the record of which is in the Journal of Convocation – were greeted with great respect (if not always with agreement). There were three areas where he played a prominent rôle in debates: canon law revision (at that time a major topic); proposals for a new baptismal rite; the new translation of the Bible. He was a member of the committees studying these subjects. In addition, he represented Convocation as a trustee of St William's College and acted as Chairman of the Lower House (i.e. the clergy) before the election of Prolocutor.

The canons which particularly interested him were those affecting worship – Canon XIV, for example, on 'Feast Days and their Observances', Canon XIX on 'Morning and Evening Prayer in Cathedral Churches', when he asserted the importance of the 'fullness of the liturgical round',[1] and Canon XXVIII on the Bidding Prayer. The last of these led Milner to resist successfully a proposal by the Bishop of Sheffield (Leslie Hunter) supported by the Dean of Chester (Michael McCausland Gibbs) that the prayer should be abandoned on grounds of its being 'out of date'. Milner's response was that charges of 'out of date' implied a likely change every decade: 'There was a certain grandeur of language which might be called out of date but which, he preferred to think, taken it was discreetly used, was never out of date.' To adapt, not to abandon, was the right policy.

The revision of Canon Law, over which the Convocation expended much time and labour, was managed in the house of clergy by Canon G. W. O. Addleshaw, Secretary of the Canon Law Commission, Canon Treasurer of the Minster, who was very learned in that field. He and Milner sometimes differed. On 17 January 1952, Addleshaw was supported on a matter concerning the position of the font in spite of his 'ecclesiological history [being] rather gravely at fault'.[2]

On the baptismal rite Milner took a strong line in favour of a simpler order. His persistence – and he never ceased to urge reform – eventually led to a serious disagreement with the Liturgical Commission,[3] the establishment of which he described as a 'counsel of despair',[4] though he accepted membership. He thought that Convocation, rather than such a body, was the best channel for effecting liturgical reform, and that joining with Canterbury was unwise, for it might involve the cutting out of the North! The speech was greeted with applause, but the vote was lost. It was one of the occasions when the observer suspects that emotive pleas on one ground (in this case loyalty to the North) were a screen for the real reason (in this case anxiety lest the York baptismal rite should not be accepted). Moreover, he affirmed, fearful of precipitate Commission decisions:

1. *Journal of Convocation*, January, 1948, p. 85.
2. p. 98. Milner accepted the Addleshavian amendment.
3. see below pp. 28–29.
4. October 1954, p. 107.

'Really good construction of common prayer needs time, for what one thought decent after a hard day's work looked rotten on the morrow, and not infrequently was rotten'.[1]

All through the debates on the baptismal rite Milner pressed for intelligibility, simplicity, the kind of phraseology which would convey the meaning of the Sacrament without disavowing its mystery. Simplicity was not the same as the prosaic, and Milner in a very forthright speech protested:

After hours of debate everyone had come to see the fact that, if the service were deprived of all that could not be understood, it ceased to be a sacrament and certainly would be deprived of anything that might be called numinous'.[2]

He was particularly concerned with the preface to the rite, and, in commenting on a draft, did not hesitate to speak of 'rubbish' in the opening words to the parents, asking whether he should try a version 'with the authority of his own fountain pen'.[3] The Preface should start with something 'very comprehensible and homely',[4] he had always argued.

The history of the revision, including the activities of the joint committee with the Convocation of Canterbury (of which Milner was a member), was highly complicated, and a provisional baptismal rite, authorised by the York Convocation, did not survive. Milner persisted in pressing for the adoption of the 'York rite' even after the establishment of the Liturgical Commission. Failure to achieve this was a great disappointment, and he protested to the end of his life that he and the Bishop of Sheffield were right to oppose forms which he called 'pattern making', by which he meant forms too 'ecclesiastical', unrelated to the realities of the milieu in which infants were brought to baptism.[5]

When (16 May 1956) the Report of the Committee on the Revision of the Bible was presented to the (full) Synod, Milner referred to members of the literary panel, whom he knew intimately. The proposed new version was neither a botching nor an amending of existing translations, and he addressed himself to questions of colloquialism and contemporary speech. Rhythm was the great pitfall. It was 'a matter purely of ear and music. One must realise that, when language changed its style and colour, it also changed its rhythm . . .'[6] He then read extracts from Ezekiel 1 and 31, Exodus 2, Psalm 29, St. John 1 and Romans 8. 'We are very grateful to the Dean of York,' concluded the Archbishop (Ramsey) 'for his description of the work of translation. It is now almost 4.30'.[7]

Milner established himself as an authoritative figure in Convocation, and respect was paid to his speeches. 'A very useful lead by the Dean of York';[8] 'The Dean's scholarship and craftsmanship';[9] 'A most learned and admirable speech from the Dean of York'.[10] These, and others, were genuine tributes, yet it is clear that, highly regarded though he

1. *ibid.*, p. 109
2. *Journal*, 25 May, 1950, p. 116.
3. *ibid.*, p. 123.
4. *Journal*, May 1946, p. 81.
5. *Journal*, January 1962, p. 117.
6. *Journal*, pp. 25–26.
7. *ibid.*, p. 26.
8. October, 1944, p. 31.
9. October, 1945, p. 33.
10. *ibid.*, p. 62.

was, he could not always convince Convocation, and over the Baptism rite he failed in the end to win a battle for which he had fought long and hard. Nevertheless over the years he contributed with care and scholarship to debates, thus maintaining the tradition of learned deans active in the national councils of the Church.

Schools occupied a good deal of Milner's time, and inspired his devotion and very practical help. The Choir School at King's had been a great joy to him, and his benign influence there is emphasised by the author of that school's history.

'The harshness and boredom of (Head Master) Jelf's régime, however, was mitigated by the substantial beneficial interest in the pupils shown by Eric Milner-White, who inspired more affection from King's pupils than any other teacher in the school's history . . . He himself taught the scripture lessons to the senior forms with a liveliness and informality that left a lasting impression on minds otherwise dulled by painstaking note learning and formal written exercises. It was for work out of the classroom, however, that Milner-White will always be lovingly remembered by the boarder and chorister pupils of his day. He was, in adult company, of a shy and nervous disposition and said little. All this disappeared when he was with children. In their presence he was 'smiling, sympathetic, bubbling over with humour, taking the boys for walks and encouraging rather than discouraging them'. He had a naturally excellent rapprochement with them, taught them largely by example to show a greater degree of charity and kindness and had an understanding of the rebellious, badly behaved, and perhaps 'misunderstood' boy. He visited the school every Sunday evening, when he took the boys for walks, joined in games of cricket, told stories or simply talked to groups of them . . . His immense influence on choristers was shared by other pupils who attended the confirmation classes which he began. It had previously been agreed by successive Deans that preparatory school boys were too young to be confirmed, but Milner-White was a believer in early confirmation. These classes took place in his rooms in College, with tea and buns; the atmosphere was pleasant and relaxed and the positive aspects of the catechism were emphasised. The Dean instilled his set of moral values, which were the same as the Headmaster's but did it more by the positive method of making doing good attractive rather than through the negative one of fear. He was anxious to keep in touch with those confirmed and often did so, well after they left the school. He generously left a sum of money to found an organ scholarship, which is awarded every two years so that the organ scholar, who holds his award for three years, works with the outgoing organist, and in his last year smoothes the entry of the next student. More than one brilliant musical career has started on this rung of the ladder.'[1]

At York that degree of intimacy could not be matched, and the social milieu was much less uniform.

Although Milner's active interest in independent schools extended to distant parts of the Province, his immediate responsibility, with the Chapter, was the Minster Choir School (now called the Minster School) with its premises in Deangate,[2], and at that time providing education for choristers and probationers only. The Head Master, George Arthur Scaife, undoubtedly was an effective, if idiosyncratic, teacher, though somewhat of a martinet, insistent upon rigorous adherence to points of discipline. The staff consisted of himself and an assistant, Miss

1. Robert Henderson, *History of King's College School*, 1981, pp. 61–2.
2. Now occupying adjacent premises also.

E. B. Whyte, an excellent teacher less given than Scaife to *fortissimo* admonition and rebuke. Milner did not hesitate to use the word 'great' of Scaife, and perhaps we can understand the generosity of the epithet of one who had given his life to the school. (Scaife's uninhibited and emphatic outbursts against offenders were in marked contrast to his restrained demeanour on the appearance of the Dean – sincere deference to authority, not sycophancy.) When he was awarded the M.B.E., it was a natural assumption that Milner had had a decisive hand in the recommendation.

But Milner, on Scaife's retirement in 1951, was aware of a need for a change, chiefly in the broadening of the curriculum; less aware, perhaps, of the desirability of changing 'chalk and talk' (however telling in Scaife's own style) into newer methods of exchange between teacher and pupil. The choice of the next Head Master was therefore crucial. In such appointments a Dean's voice is of necessity paramount, as he has to work comfortably with the Head Master and ensure that that officer can co-operate with others alongside whom he has to function. Personal relations in cathedral bodies are matters of particular delicacy. In the event Milner made his own choice – and the Chapter's formal assent did not disguise it. D. V. Hewitt was an old chorister (reared by Scaife) and a Kingsman. He was also appointed Vicar-Choral. His experience was that of the parochial ministry, and it might well be asked whether professional advice should have been sought on possible candidates with a teaching background.[1] The appointment illustrated Milner's very personal way of proceeding in such matters.

He was assiduous in getting to know the choristers, noting their progress, and encouraging them. His predecessor, Dean Bate, had not failed to help and advise, as the present writer can testify, but it was with Milner a constant joy to mark the development (including the musical standard) of the boys. He generously furthered their continuing education by endowing (Milner-White) scholarships at St Peter's School, as did Edward Long, an old Peterite.

At St Peter's he became (*ex officio*) Chairman of the Governors.[2] The then Head Master, John Dronfield, in his obituary notice of Milner said that he was best in dealing with the problems of the individual, though his sermons were described as 'memorable, . . . models of diction, prepared with meticulous care and lightened with flashes of sly humour'. One sermon on 'courtesy' was said by one housemaster to have made such an impression that many requests were made for a transcript, and it was printed.[3]

Milner effectively drew together the school and the Minster, not least by involving St Peter's in the Epiphany Procession (from 1947). The other York school with which he was closely associated, the College for Girls, neighbour to the Song School, was a member of the Church Schools Company. Milner became Chairman of the local

1. M-W Papers I.1–5, include references to changes in the school's standards of accommodation, to Hewitt's appointment and to Scaife's pension of £250 p.a.
2. M-W Papers, IV.6.
3. *The Peterite*, January 1952, part 329, p. 26.

Council. Inevitable lack of repair during the War called for urgent action, and the central body had to be convinced that it was right to acquire adjacent property, demolish it and so provide new (and expanded) accommodation. Items which the Company deemed inessential were financed locally, and there Milner was an effective adviser. The schemes included a small chapel (still in use), which has a window by Harry Stammers portraying the Annunciation. In the background is a Nativity scene, with the Dean represented as the third shepherd. As with St Peter's School, the commendable aim was to link the York College for Girls more closely with the Minster. The effective link was the Dean himself, regarded somewhat with awe, but greatly appreciated for his financial acumen and for the evidence of his pastoral care in the appointment of a visiting chaplain, with a regular celebration of the Eucharist. The office he devised for Speech Day is no longer used: a Milnerian composition may well be unsuited to the temper of later generations.

From 1945 Milner was Provost of the Northern Division of the Woodard Corporation, an office which in some respects ranks above that of the heads of the respective schools. The Provostship involved much travelling and considerable application. Queen Margaret's School, originally at Scarborough, is at Escrick, about seven miles from York. Milner took one look at a somewhat derelict estate dairy building there and said, 'I think I can make this a very beautiful chapel'. This he did, and enriched it with vestments and frontals (a court garment of a princess was transformed into a red chasuble). There were additions of buildings and land, transactions about which were made under Milner's guidance. His installation in Chapel was a splendid occasion, surpassed only by Solemn Eucharist of Thanksgiving in the Minster on 3 June 1961, for the school's golden jubilee. Like other schools in the Division, Queen Margaret's was given an official grant of arms, a move initiated by Milner. At St Ethelburga's, Harrogate, there were similar modifications and additions to buildings. Queen Mary's at Duncombe Park, Helmsley, a junior school, was threatened in 1960 with closure, when the then Earl of Feversham decided not to renew the lease in 1966. Milner invited the Earl to meet the Woodard Chapter, the school was reprieved, and a new lease granted.

Two more girls' schools,[1] Brentwood near Southport, and Waverley at Huddersfield, were brought under the Woodard umbrella at Milner's instigation, and at both he demonstrated a characteristic combination of idealism over aims and practical sagacity over buildings. Personal generosity was again in evidence, as it was at the King's School, Tynemouth, which came to occupy a very special place in Milner's affection. Brentwood and Waverley were designated Queen Winifred's and Queen Philippa's respectively (on the former Milner bestowed the motto 'Courtesy is of Christ' – who but he would have devised such a maxim?).

---

1.   M-W Papers IV.4/5. Scarborough College was also considered (IV.5), but nothing came of it. Queen Margaret's is no longer a Woodard School.

All the girls' schools had to be Queens: Tynemouth (for boys; formerly Tynemouth Grammar School) was renamed the King's School. Once again a chapel was created, and buildings were added or improved. The Woodard Chapter were persuaded to take on this school, and Milner contributed with immense financial generosity towards the implementation of his schemes. The appointment of Head Master he virtually took into his own hands.[1] The Reverend Malcolm Nicholson (King's and Cuddesdon) himself described his appointment as 'curious', as his offices hitherto had been parochial and archidiaconal. He had no illusions about Milner's *modus operandi*, and combined affection and gratitude for his work with reservations about the methods of pursuing it.[2] In 1959, the Head Master was in trouble when the contract for work in Priory Park was placed, authorised only by Milner, who failed to rescue him when he was accused of precipitate action. 'One paid the price for being Milner's trusted agent,' he wrote.[3] As with the other schools, a coat of arms was devised and a motto bestowed: '*Moribus Civilis*', which, apparently, came from the description of 'our King', Oswin, in Bede.

To no school did Milner give such detailed personal attention, visiting it regularly even when far from well. His outstanding characteristic here, as with the other schools with which he was associated, was the combination of idealism and practicality.

That combination was evident in Milner's important activities in the City of York, the first being the inauguration of the Civic Trust.

In Cambridge, Milner had interested himself in the appearance of buildings, not least in shops and their signs. Shop fascia, he believed passionately, called for artistic sensibility. At York, once the War was over, the time was ripe for an initiative to preserve the City's architectural heritage and to enhance the beauty of what Milner called the artistic capital of the North. The creation of the Civic Trust in July 1946 enabled these ambitions to be fulfilled, guarding against the dangers of hurried and ill-considered development, as York emerged, somewhat dishevelled, from the War years.

The Archbishop (C. F. Garbett) formally proposed the setting up of the Trust,[4] and G. M. Trevelyan addressed the opening meeting. John Bowes Morrell, Oliver Sheldon and Noel Terry, along with Milner, were the prime movers in the enterprise, and Milner and Sheldon were appointed Joint Honorary Secretaries, Morrell Chairman. The Trust badge, a 1423 assay mark, was Milner's choice.

It is important to stress that the Trust, initially an Association, came into being for 'preservation, amenity and design'.[5] Conservation was but one part of the aim: encouragement of good design was the positive objective, and to that end the Trust was committed 'ardently' to co-operate with the City Council. (Milnerian adverbs are as characteristic as Milnerian subjunctives.) The reader of the first Report, 50 years on,

1. Though it had the approval of Lord Halifax; 2. Malcolm Nicholson, *Milner and his Benjamin*, tells the story of the foundation of the King's School. (no date and no pagination), and the *King's School Magazine*, Summer Term, 1963; 3. *Milner and his Benjamin*; 4. 18 July, 1946; 5. *Annual Report*, 1946–7, p. 1, gives Milner's summary of aims. The original full title is given on p. 1 of the preliminary document.

is impressed, not only by the principles which animated the sponsors of the Trust, but by their grasp of practical matters – the need to work closely with the civic authorities, the setting up of a streets and buildings committee and provision for efficient administrative arrangements. Milner's first action was to meet the City Engineer: the aim to 'build without controversy the City Beautiful' was not hindered for lack of realism in the means of achieving it.

As the annual reports of the Minster Friends are a major record of the history of the building and its furnishings, so the annual reports of the Civic Trust tell the story of preservation, amenity and design in York. On both Milner set his seal, not only by a distinctive literary style, but by evident determination fully to achieve the purposes for which both bodies existed. The success of the Trust, and Milner's many initiatives within it, depended on a partnership of founders and civic authorities. This came about: mutual confidence was assured, and Milner was acknowledged as the authoritative voice.

The annual reports tell of major developments in the cultural life of the City: the 'new birth' of the Art Gallery, the Summer Schools in Archive and Architectural Studies, then the York Institute of Architectural Study, the Borthwick Institute of Historical Research; all under the benign encouragement and active support of the Trust, which from its first days fostered plans for the establishment of a University. Then there were artistic events which had the Trust's warm encouragement: the Festival of Britain (1951), the York Festivals and the Mystery Plays, which continued after 1951.

But the most characteristic achievements of the enterprise were the improvements in artistic standards, in relation to buildings, great and small, to noble streets like Micklegate, and to the lay-out of gardens and open spaces. A shop fascia, a refuse bin, an inn sign, a bus shelter – none escaped the Decanal eye, and expressions in the Reports like 'flawlessly wrought' (of York craftsmanship) and 'the redemption of Hungate' were unmistakably the mark of the Decanal pen. On 93 Micklegate, the 1948–9 Report declared that 'externally [it] must be the most attractive fish and chip shop in existence'. Interiors had careful attention – for instance an Adam chimney-piece in the Mansion House, where also the restoration of window bars was warmly commended. Although Milner had a vision of Stonegate as one of the finest streets in Europe, he also looked with enthusiasm to new development, recording 'a fine new street' envisaged in the Stonebow plan.

To the West of the Church of St Michael-le-Belfrey there is, let into the ground, a stone (well lettered by Milnerian standards). It bids us remember Eric Milner-White. It is rightly sited – hard by the Minster, but also at the heart of the City to which he gave so much in affection and artistic creativity.

From the inception of the Civic Trust the prospect of a University at York had been in the minds of the Trust's promoters. The first annual report makes reference to it. Milner, who was an enthusiastic supporter, was elected Chairman of the Trust's Academic Development Committee. That committee's (independent) successor was the York Academic Trust, of which he was also Chairman. The papers in the Minster Library[1] testify to his conviction, agreed by the Academic Trust, that the University should be collegiate: Cambridge was in his mind, not only in that connection, but also in his concern for the visual character of the surroundings (what he would *not* have called the 'campus'!) As to the faculties, theology was not considered, in the knowledge that existing university provision was adequate for the need. Milner was anxious that, in addition to the humanities, more particularly history and architecture, there should be strong departments in the natural and social sciences. He intervened effectively in one debate on the plans for the buildings (by Robert Matthew, Johnson-Marshall and Partners), resisting conservative opinion that they should be in the style of the Gothic revival. (Lord James of Rusholme, the first Vice-Chancellor, confirms the crucial character of Milner's intervention.) The plans, he stated in a memorable speech, met the conditions laid down by Sir Henry Wotton, the Jacobean humanist who wrote the *Elements of Architecture*, – Commodity, Firmness and Delight.

In 1959 he had invited Sir Keith Murray, Chairman of the University Grants Committee, to stay at the Deanery. It was a fruitful visit, and the York project was especially memorable in that, unlike others, it was not promoted by a local education authority, but by a group of local citizens. In the whole enterprise Milner once more had exhibited a characteristic combination of idealism with a firm grasp of practicality.[2] When he was already declining in health, he joined the Promotion Committee for the University (a committee required by the Government), the Archbishop being Chairman. Regrettably the year of the University's opening was the year of his death.

Is it too late for the University in some way to register by a suitable memorial appreciation of Milner's work? He purchased a field near Heslington Church, and gave it to the University, to preserve an open space and to retain the prospect thus revealed. Such generosity, itself but one aspect of Milner's contribution over many years, deserves visible recognition.

In the foregoing account of Milner's tenure of the Deanery of York, no mention has been made of simultaneous activities beyond the Northern Province. He was an *ex officio* member of the Church Assembly, the meetings of which provided such valuable opportunity for treasure hunting in London. For some years he was one of the two Vice-Chairmen of the Central Advisory Council for the Care of Churches (previously he had learned the practicalities of a diocesan advisory committee's work through his membership of the Ely D.A.C.).

1. Especially M-W IV.1.
2. In *Towards a University*, 1967, the late Canon J. S. Purvis refers to an idea, attributed to Milner, that there should be a 'University of Britain', with a college of professors, concentrating on teaching the English (sic) way of life (*op. cit.*, p. 26). This 'vision' is referred to in the Trust's Annual Report for 1953–4, p. 4 (a residential college).

From 1943 to 1959 he was President of the Henry Bradshaw Society, which is concerned with the printing of liturgical manuscripts and rare editions of service books, particularly those which bear upon the history of the Book of Common Prayer. From 1944 to 1959 he was a member of the Advisory Council of the Victoria and Albert Museum, and in 1948 was made an Honorary Member of the Worshipful Company of Glaziers, with the Freedom of the City of London. In 1952 Archbishop Fisher gave him a Lambeth Doctorate of Divinity, and in the same year he was made C.B.E. Ten years later the University of Leeds conferred on him an honorary Doctorate of Letters. He remained a Fellow of King's and continued to fulfil his statutory duties there. Yet none of these activities circumscribed his work for York, Minster, City and Province.

1941 was a dismal year in which to start new work. Milner succeeded Herbert Newell Bate, whom a later Dean of York described as 'A Reticent Genius'.[1] His few years at York – he was installed in 1932 – were overshadowed by the economic depression of the early '30s, by the threat of war and by the onset of war itself. Bate was deeply involved in the Faith and Order Movement: he was a pioneer in ecumenical work, a key figure in the Lausanne Conference of 1927, a theologian and biblical scholar, a liturgist and a musician; to all of which fields he brought distinguished gifts. Those qualities which gave such high promise were exercised in adverse circumstances. Nevertheless, within the nine years of Bate's tenure of office more was achieved than is sometimes realised. The new Deanery was built, and, within the Minster, work started on the extensive (and expensive) restoration of the North Transept roof. The reordering of the Choir sanctuary, the restoration of St Stephen's Chapel, the provision of new vestries, the restoration and refurnishing of the Zouche Chapel and the restoration of the Saint Cuthbert window were considerable achievements. While so much in the Minster speaks of Milner, his predecessor's work must not be forgotten, nor his outstanding gifts underestimated.

Was Milner a theologian? He was certainly well read in traditional Anglican divinity – the Church Fathers and the Caroline Divines. But, as A. M. Ramsey indicated in his epilogue to the Memoir by Pare and Harris, his association with the Cambridge 'school' of High Churchmanship did not prompt him to contribute anything of consequence to theological thinking in the decade following 1910. The title of the work associated with 'a fresh exposition and defence of the Catholic faith',[2] *Essays Catholic and Critical*, sufficiently indicates the general outlook of its several authors, and to that volume, published in 1926, Milner contributed. His essay, 'The Spirit and the Church in History', is epigrammatic in style and hardly qualifies as theological exploration, let alone equals the weighty contributions of, for example, Sir Edwin Hoskyns or Will Spens.[3] As Ramsey pointed out, Milner's energies

---

1. Ronald Jasper, *Herbert Newell Bate, 1871–1941*, 1987. See also John Bate, 'Herbert Newell Bate', in the Friends *Report*, 1987.
2. 1926, Preface, p. v.
3. The point that Milner reflected on life in the Church rather than explored the theological concepts which underlay the life is startlingly evident if his essay is compared with, e.g. David Brown, 'Holy Spirit: the argument from history', in *The Divine Trinity*, 1985.

were directed to the work of the Oratory of the Good Shepherd (1913) and to the pastoral needs of undergraduates, particularly to new and urgent problems after 1918.[1] His métier was that of a counsellor and preacher rather than theological scholar, and his inspiration, after the Scriptures, were the classical Anglican divines. He published other essays, one on 'Christian Unity' in the Report of the First Anglo-Catholic Congress, 1920, and in 1929 a reply to Father Vernon, *One God and Father of All*. The latter was written jointly by Milner, Superior of the Oratory of the Good Shepherd, and Wilfred Knox, Warden of the Oratory House. These essays restate the liberal Catholic position, repudiating the Roman claims to infallibility and claiming Scriptural authority for that theological stance. Milner was more effective as preacher than as theological writer; thus 'The Incarnation and the Church', in *Catholic Sermons*,[2] is an exposition within the context of worship, the more compelling for being so.

In those areas in which Milner excelled – notably glass, the visual arts, textiles and furnishings – his knowledge was deep, his understanding scholarly. Yet it cannot be claimed that he was a theologian, or indeed historian, given exploration and research as accepted criteria for such designation,[3] and he never wrote any substantial work in those areas.

His sermons – many of which survive[4] – were carefully prepared, and were always felicitously expressed. Indeed, sometimes the richness of the language, combined with distinctive Milnerian turns of phrase, diverts attention from the message to the medium. These were by no means popular sermons, and Milner was of course entirely free from the preaching gimmicks which so often pass for the proclamation of the Gospel. The regular congregation at York Minster, however, might have found some of the Dean's utterances somewhat beyond their understanding: it might even be questioned whether all the hearers would understand '*damnosa hereditas*' which he used of sin, or 'the glories of the New Eternal Covenant of God' with its promise of the release from bondage to that unhappy condition.[5] But the character of the style, with its echoes of the Caroline divines, must not cloud the quality of these discourses, rooted in Scripture, in the writings of saints and in personal meditation. Sermons on 'special occasions', for example that on the death of King George VI,[6] while not in the least announcing the unexpected, are never trite. For a National Day of Prayer he dwelt on the spiritual issues of the War, recalling on another occasion what must indeed have risen from his own experience in an earlier conflict, 'the filthiness of modern war'.[7]

Two of the surviving sermons are of special interest. The first, delivered in St James's, Piccadilly, was a memorial address for F. C. Eeles,[8] on the text, Isaiah 33.17, 'Thine eyes shall see the king in his beauty.' It says much of Milner himself: 'For the loveliness he sought went

1. Ramsey in *op. cit.*, p. 102;   2. ed. Humphrey Beevor, 1932, pp. 89–93;   3. Milner wrote an introduction to E. S. Duckett, *Latin Writers of the Fifth Century*, 1930. It shows learning rather than critical scholarship;   4. Archives, King's College, Cambridge, L3 (Services at York Minster), and N4 (War Sermons 1940–5);   5. Lent 2, 1949 (L3);   6. N4, 3, 15 February 1952;   7. L/3/2 (1941 only noted);   8. From 1924 for many years Secretary to the Central Council for the Care of Churches.

further than temple or worship; he sought the King himself in his beauty. The King, glorious in His lowly birth, the King majestic in His sordid death, the King of grace and peace eternal adored by the shining ones of Heaven, feeding His own on earth with His own life'.[1] The same text from Isaiah was used for the memorial address for Robert Thompson, 'minister of craftsmanship and the dignity of beauty in the house of God',[2] recalling Thompson's work 'in my great Minster'. God perceived through beauty was a *leitmotif* of Milner's ministry, and the recollection of his ordering of acts of worship raises the question of his reputation as a liturgist.

In the Preface to the new edition of the Cuddesdon Office Book, in 1940, the then Principal, Eric Graham, referred to 'the old student whose liturgical skill and diligent care has made this Office Book what it is.' About half a century later a similar tribute was paid by Canon Donald Gray, who described Milner as a 'highly competent liturgist and skilled author of collects and prayers'.[3] Milner's reputation in the Church rests largely on successive books of prayers and on the creation of forms of worship for 'special' occasions. His interests, however, were not confined to the composition of prayers and the ordering of services: the structure and language of formal liturgy engaged his attention, chiefly the rite of baptism.

The Hours of Daily Prayer in the Cuddesdon Office Book (1940) open with the words, *'Non clamor sed amor psallit in aure Dei.'* Dr. Owen Chadwick explains the origin of this insertion:

'On the way to Assisi in 1907 Philip Loyd (then Vice-Principal, later Bishop successively of Nasik and St Albans) and E. Milner-White (then about to be a student) found the text inlaid along the cornice of the priests' stalls round the apse of the Church of Spello, Umbria.'[4]

That text was the foundation of Milner's liturgical work. The sources from which he derived inspiration were succinctly described by Dr. Chadwick:

'Though he used the ancient western liturgies and appreciated to the full the Tractarian wish to adopt their beauties . . . he lifted his eyes to wider horizons. Though he studied the models of many centuries, he looked first, perhaps, to the prayers of the early Carolines of Lancelot Andrewes, Jeremy Taylor, Laud, Donne, Traherne. These men drew, like the Tractarians, from the ancient liturgies, but often from the Greek liturgies rather than the western sacramentaries and breviaries. Milner-White had steeped himself in this tradition. This catholic trend was reinforced by Graham's contribution. Graham was familiar with the ancient Greek liturgies and with Andrewes . . . the Caroline tradition (among a diversity of sources) was the principal influence. . . . The influence upon the office-book of 1940 was a new breadth, a catholic range of prayer.'[5]

Milner himself described the aim of the revision as 'a judicious blend of uses.'[6] In its preparation Graham had been somewhat alarmed that

1. N4/6, 9 November, 1954.
2. N4/5, dated April.
3. *Earth and Altar*, Alcuin Club Collections, 68, 1986, p. 47.
4. *The Founding of Cuddesdon*, 1954, p. 137.
5. *op. cit.*, pp. 134–5.
6. Robert T. Holtby, *Eric Graham*, 1967, p. 36.

the book might become a monument to the men of the 17th century rather than of practical use to those of the 20th.[1] The exuberance of Milner's style had to be curbed, and he loyally abode by the judgement of the Cuddesdon officers. 'I enclose a Penitential act which I have extracted, with scarcely a change from sermon 107 of Donne. It seems to me so good that it were worth your considering it' (characteristic Milnerian subjunctive).[2] What he called the 'Long Delayed Book' was indeed a work of excellence, not least in its Eucharistic devotions, which Milner thought most profitable, 'with age-long liturgy in their substance'.[3]

Reference has already been made to the radical criticism of the Book of Common Prayer made by Milner in the circumstances of the *Church in the Furnace*. He had been distressed by the widespread ignorance of the Faith ('the great festivals spell torture and sorrow to the keen priest').[4] While acknowledging that some archaism in liturgical language promoted dignity, he thought that the rest was unsympathetic. The office of baptism should be four times as short and ten times more comprehensible, and additional collects and other material were required. The time of celebrations of the Holy Communion needed reconsideration, and he urged much more teaching *through the eye*. Altogether, a gigantic task of instruction was laid on the chaplains (rebels and 'revolutionaries'[5]), to remedy a state of affairs brought about by a supine clergy. 'The matter in hand is not personal preference, not even liturgical propriety, but the facts and lessons of France'.[6]

The War papers were all destroyed, and in due course the Prayer Book regained a central place in Milner's regard. The desperate urgency of ministry in the conditions of trench warfare had passed, though the underlying problems of ignorance and secularisation remained. While the immediate reaction to the one disappeared, Milner never lost sight of the other, and continued to plead both for special services and for prayers additional to those in the Prayer Book. He set out his considered view on special services (describing them as a 'liturgical need') in the 'York Quarterly' of February 1959, in which he argued for building on the foundation of historic liturgies and against their *imitation*. As to structure, the responses must be clear, the movement precise, the postures right, and the congregational element definite. He claimed that the Festival of Nine Lessons and Carols at Christmas, adapted from Truro, fulfilled these conditions fully. As to forms, those which are *known* are all important – the Lord's Prayer, the Creed, for example. Other historic forms would be used in new contexts – for instance the scriptural sentences at the beginning of the daily office. Lessons would be a sequence. The chief point in this article is thus expressed: 'The purpose of the particular Act must be crystal clear. When such a service is requested from the Minster, I usually begin by asking the promoters, "What is it you are wanting to say to God?" And from that moment

1. Pare and Harris, *op. cit.*, pp. 42–3.
2. Holtby, *op. cit.*, pp. 34–5.
3. *ibid.*, p. 35.
4. *op. cit.*, p. 199.
5. *ibid.*, p. 176.
6. *ibid.*, p. 201. Canon Gray comments on Milner's wartime views in *Earth and Altar*.

the whole approach is apt to change'.[1] These were the principles which inspired Milner's authorship of very many special services, some of which – Advent, Christmas, Epiphany, Harvest, have become widely known. Any tinkering with the order by clergymen in the cause of brevity or popularisation endangers those principles. Moreover, Milner's practice in the conduct of special services matched his ideals. Processions had to be correctly marshalled; the dress and posture of all ministers had to be appropriate; dignity (and not fuss) had to mark all ceremony. Nothing less than perfection would suffice for public worship, including the condition of the habits of ministers. For the Royal wedding he adjured the members of the Minster Chapter to appear in choir robes of 'snowy white'.[2]

Milner's first published reflections on occasional prayers appeared shortly after the rejection by Parliament of the Revised Prayer book, 'The Occasional Prayers in the 1928 Book reconsidered'.[3] He criticised the collection for being inadequate in its provision for modern need and lacking distinction in form and expression. The eminent liturgical scholar, E. C. Ratcliff, had some adverse criticism of Milner's comments:

'Certain of Mr Milner-White's suggestions will command general agreement. . . . His preference for Laud's prayer to the State of the intercession for the British Empire (in the '28 Book) will be generally shared; but few will prefer his mangled version of it to Laud's fine original. The necessity of some of Mr. Milner-White's needs, however, and the rightness of some of his provisions, may be questioned. Should the well-to-do, for instance, be singled out as special objects of prayerful solicitude, as in the intercession 'For the Right use of Possessions', unless we ask also that those not burdened with the responsibilities of the wealthy may be moved to discharge their own?'[4]

Yet, Ratcliff acknowledged, Milner claimed no more than the making of suggestions:

'The usefulness of his book is considerable, and his detailed and irrefutable criticisms have made it impossible for this section of the proposed Prayer Book to re-appear in a future revision without drastic amendment and alteration.'[5]

In the same volume Milner himself contributed an article, 'Modern Prayers and their Writers'. Here he recalled the 'incomparable' character of the Prayer Book, yet 'Supreme still in quality, it had become, by the working out of its own good influence, too small in range. Old age, new learning and liturgical scholarship together destroyed its authority, not its beauty.'[6]

The reader of that article must be struck by the immense learning of its author in the field of devotional literature, and his command of the wide range of sources outside the Prayer Book, universal in scope. In the Bible and Prayer Book in Cranmer's time, the Church indeed had 'gained a tongue meet for celestial service'.[7] Within the ensuing

1.   p. 10. King's Carols not 'a sentimental concert' (ibid.).
2.   M-W Papers XIII, 2, 8 June 1961.
3.   1929.
4.   E. C. Ratcliff, 'The Choir Offices', in *Liturgy and Worship*, 1932, p. 278.
5.   *ibid.*, p. 279.
6.   *op. cit.*, in *Liturgy and Worship*, p. 758.
7.   *ibid.*, p. 751.

tradition were the Caroline divines, and, above all the influences on Anglican devotion, 'towers the greatest book of private devotion that Christian and Catholic piety has begotten, the *Preces Privatae* of Lancelot Andrewes',[1] which had set 'the unofficial prayers of the Church a standard of order and content which is unsurpassable'.[2] From the 17th century Milner passed to the 19th, recalling how the Oxford Movement had enriched devotional literature. He welcomed modern forms – for instance, those of Toc H and the B.B.C. – provided they met the criteria which he applied in another connection: 'The experiments at Liverpool Cathedral,' he wrote, 'will be valuable if they teach discrimination between devotions borne on the passing winds of novelty or special occasion and those which have catholic substance and endurance'.[3]

So came Milner's own notable contributions, the first (with B. T. D. Smith), *Cambridge Offices and Orisons*, in 1921, for public devotion, simple offices based on the day hours of the Western Church, with a corresponding series of intercessions and litanies. Then *Memorials Upon Several Occasions* was published anonymously in 1933, the third edition entitled *After the Third Collect* issued in 1952 (authorship then acknowledged), with the limited aim 'to help the parish priest to make fuller use of the "second part of the prayers" at Matins and, above all, Evensong, along accustomed liturgical lines'.[4] The index of sources sufficiently points to the breadth of those writers of whom Milner had written in his essay on modern prayers (and includes his own work under the heading 'King's College, Cambridge', and in the 1938 revision his wonderful prayer for peace).

Of subsequent works the most widely familiar is *Daily Prayer*, published (with G. W. Briggs) in 1941, and issued as a Pelican Book in 1959. It is a selection of prayers for public, private and school worship, arranged by subjects and drawn from many sources, though chiefly from 'the prayers of our own countrymen'.[5] The Appendix on 'The Form and Structure of Prayers' (from the Cambridgeshire Syllabus of Religious Teaching for Schools) is a statement which, with brevity and clarity, sets out the principles which guided Milner in his choice and adaptation of prayers and the ways in which corporate prayer can be enriched. The Appendix ends with a paragraph which might profitably be inscribed in the notebook (better, the mind) of every minister who conducts public worship:

'Amongst modern prayers much discrimination is needed. Those which seek to impress themselves by romantic and high-flown language, such as "gallant and high-hearted happiness," should be used at most only occasionally; artificiality must be avoided. For the young, prayers ought usually to be brief and direct; but that is no reason why they should be commonplace or dull. Finally, however good or indifferent the prayer may be, it may be ruined or redeemed by the way in which it is said.'[6]

Milner's own enunciation exemplified the last point – careful attention

1. *ibid.*
2. *ibid.*, p. 752.
3. *ibid.*, p. 760.
4. Foreword, p. v.
5. Preface, p. 9.
6. Pelican Edition, 1959, p. 202.

to diction and evident feeling for rhythm. The frequent practice by officiants of adding 'Amen' to their public prayers would have seemed to him a failure to understand an important element of corporate worship, that of *response*.

What now seems a strange lapse was the inclusion in *Daily Prayer* of a prayer by R. L. Stevenson[1] among the 'Prayers of Famous Men and Women', suffering, as it does, from 'romantic and high-flown language', the aspiration of 'good chaps'.

A Cambridge Bede Book (1936) was dedicated *'Matribus Dilectissimis'*, King's and Annie Booth Milner-White. The prayers were new, 'but not on that account original', and were inspired chiefly by the Caroline writers. In the Preface, Milner laid stress on the value of the collect form: 'It is the form of vocal prayer which can best bear pushing upon and frequent repetition: a good collect should be a brief but full meditation'.[2]

A Procession of Passion Prayers, marshalled (*sic*) by Eric Milner-White, was published in 1950. It fills the need for a wider range of prayers on Christ's death than that offered by the Prayer Book, and avoids the pitfalls of modern devotional manuals, most of which 'are too subjective and emotional for an Englishman to use profitably; and in structure, expression and balance leave much to be desired'.[3] Milner would have been gratified to learn that one of the prayers – 'The Way of the Cross' – which he included appears in the Alternative Service Book as the Collect for the Fourth Sunday before Easter. From its original author, W. H. Huntingdon, it had passed into the American Prayer Book.[4]

The last two books of prayers – 'Aspirations, Acts and Prayers' – were published when Milner felt his life was coming to its end – *My God, My Glory* in 1954 and *Let Grace Reign* in 1960, the latter dedicated to the Vicars Choral of York Minster 'with my deep love and gratitude'.

Milner as a writer of prayers deserves particular attention not least because what he wrote says so much of what he was. The language and style reflect the sources with which he was very closely familiar, but his personal stamp is evident in both. If occasionally touches of the precious supervene, it is nevertheless beyond doubt that the prayers maintain the dignity of good English, commendable reticence, and that sense of rhythm which Milner deemed essential, a quality often lacking in modern revision, particularly of collects.

In the wider sphere of (formal) liturgical revision Milner was made Chairman of a Commission appointed by Archbishop Fisher to prepare a report on 'Commemoration of Saints and Heroes of the Faith in the Anglican Communion'. The (unanimous) report was published in 1957, in preparation for the Lambeth Conference of the following year. That such observances had been abused was no reason for rejecting them;

---

1. *ibid.*, p. 196.
2. p. viii.
3. Introduction, p. xii.
4. See Adrian Leak, 'Eric Milner-White's Prayers', Friends of York Minster *Report*, 1984, p. 23, an article of distinction.

'Kalendrical observance is a living fact and issue'.[1] There was a reference to the revision of the Kalendar in the Cuddesdon Office Book, with which Milner had of course been associated, and it was recommended that a provincial or diocesan synod should be deemed the natural instrument for additions or subtractions and for appropriate liturgical provision.

Milner proved himself a good chairman, who held together a diverse body of people. When, later, the Liturgical Commission occupied itself with the Calendar Question, they took some note of what the (Milner) Commission had said, but virtually ignored the distinction between Saints and Worthies on which they had insisted.[2]

Milner's interest in Prayer Book reform, apart from his special concern with occasional prayers, has already been indicated in the account given of his interventions in the York Convocation debates, where he was prominent in discussion on the revision of the baptismal rite. Here the story was less happy, and the outcome a disappointment to him.

He set out his general ideas in an article in *Theology* in October 1943, 'Prayer Book Revision'.[3] Beginning with the need for revision and for clearer directive rubrics, he lamented the excessive variations in current practice, as indeed also the signs of the decline of a sense of liturgy and of historic Christian devotion. A time for ordered experiment was needed to frame a prayer book guaranteeing worship which was 'scriptural, historical, seasonal and structural'.[4] Diction and dignity should not fall below the standard of 1662 on the grounds that 'august standard of language arises immediately from the august use to which it ministers. . . . Both words and silence are sacramentals of worship'.[5] He again stressed the importance of rhythm.

For Milner, revision ought to be a familiar and continuous factor in Church life, and it should be pursued on the principle that liturgical worship is, properly, conservative, but never static. (1928, he thought, had tried too much – including 76 pages of preliminary matter!) He advocated some small changes in the 1662 communion office, with permissive variation in the order of the Canon.

The revision of the baptismal rite proved to be a contentious issue. The details have been retailed by the late Dean of York, R. C. D. Jasper, in his book *The Development of the Anglican Liturgy, 1662–1980*.[6] In his 1943 Article, Milner had advocated the establishment of a liturgical commission, presumably in the light of his conviction that revision should be a continuous process. When, in October 1954, the Convocation agreed a Liturgical Commission, he opposed it, describing it as a 'counsel of despair.' Nevertheless, he joined it, and was very helpful – so Dean Jasper records[7] – when the Commission began its work: a memorandum of 30 hand-written pages on occasional prayers and thanksgivings was evidence of that. The difficulties arose, however, over the proposed baptismal rite. Milner and Canon Ernest Evans strove

1. *Report*, p. 39.
2. Letter to the author from the Bishop of Chichester (E. W. Kemp), Secretary of the Commission.
3. Vol. XLVI, No. 280.
4. *ibid.*, p. 219;   5. *ibid.*, p. 219;   6. 1989;   7. Jasper, *op.cit.*, p. 213.

to secure the adoption of the York rite, but the Commission in January 1958 accepted a draft prepared by Canon Arthur Couratin. Couratin's draft satisfied the Commission on theological and liturgical grounds, was much more radical than the York draft, and assumed as the norm the administration of Baptism within the Eucharist. Milner and Evans produced a 'minority' report (hardly that, as the 'majority' had not seen it) though eventually the dissenting documents were circulated, and, Dean Jasper complained, 'The Archbishop (Fisher) appeared to be treating the Minority as a separate Commission with direct access to Lambeth.'[1] Milner attended his last meeting of the Commission in December 1958, and thereafter sent regular apologies for absence, though his opposition continued. The championship of Convocation (as against the Liturgical Commission) as the authoritative body was at least paradoxical, given the formal (national) status of the Liturgical Commission.

Milner's name, then, is chiefly associated with the sensitive composition and adaptation of prayers and the creation of 'special' forms of worship. While it can be said justly that from time to time elegance of expression captures attention at some cost to content, there is no doubt of the supreme value of his prayers for public and private use. He filled a great need for 'occasional' prayers, and their literary quality is what it is because of their author's deep understanding of Anglican spirituality and, particularly, his sense of the 'august' *standard* set by the Prayer Book. Of his 'special' forms, the Festival of Nine Lessons is best known, the Advent Carol Service most profoundly conceived, eye with ear used together to enact the theme of 'light'.

One of the former Chaplains of King's[2] has drawn attention to Milner's use of pairs of words, to achieve emphasis by repetition of thought, exemplified in the Bidding Prayer of the Festival of Nine Lessons: 'care and delight . . . heart and mind . . . read and mark . . . peace and goodwill . . . the sick and them that mourn . . .'. It was not only a literary device: it was an instance of the music – and rhythm – of language.

It is evident that Milner was by no means an opponent of liturgical innovation, but the question presses very heavily fifty years after his arrival in York: how does the language of revision accord with 'the august use to which it ministers'? Within the field of his special interests he can rightly be accounted an outstanding liturgist. Strangely – the York baptismal rite apart – while familiar with historic liturgies, he made no contribution of significance to the revision of regular forms of public worship, notably the Eucharist. Developments there – including oecumenical discussion – matured after his death.

'What do you want to say to God?' The supremacy of the collect form; the importance of silence; the dignity of language for the dignity and duty of worship: we need to remember these principles and recall

---

1. *ibid.*, p. 220.
2. Canon P. C. Magee.

the 'proper liturgical response to the issues of "this day and age" is a reticence which does not distract us from a greater Day and Age'.[1]

Milner's professional relationships were marked by contrast, and revealed the complex aspects of his character. With successive Archbishops of York his deference to the office was matched by regard for its holder. He had been at York but a short time when William Temple was translated to Canterbury. On a preliminary visit to York, his successor, Cyril Garbett, found the Dean 'very friendly'.[2] The Minster thrilled him, and he acquired a growing affection and admiration for the Dean'.[3] The next Archbishop, Michael Ramsey, had been taught by Milner at the King's Choir School, and for him there was unstinted, not to say uncritical, admiration. On Ramsey's own translation to Canterbury, Milner wrote a letter quoted by Dr. Owen Chadwick in his obituary notice, '+ Michael Ebor', printed in the 1989 Report of the Friends of York Minster,

'Beloved Archbishop,
   With your departure for Canterbury for me the Golden Age of the Church departs also. That does not mean that I could easily have borne any other figure in St. Augustine's Chair than your own. And I can only hope – and pray – that the overwhelming labour of the Chair will fail to damp, divert or exhaust the fresh winds of Holy Spirit which God will send us all through you. These are few words, and my heart is too full to say more. Except that in the few years – or days – left to me, I shall always regard the Minster as your Church and myself as your son at York – and your Father at Canterbury.'[4]

Donald Coggan succeeded Ramsey, and Milner enthroned him. He speaks of 'a very happy relationship with Eric',[5] though there was a very short time between his arrival and Milner's death.

It is good if there is *rapport* between dean and bishop – a relationship friendly, trusting and co-operative, and such was the case in Milner's time. Archbishops are too preoccupied to concern themselves closely in the affairs of their cathedral, and there was no formal Visitation in the Milner years. More difficult – and often intractable – are the relationships within the cathedral body itself, members and officers. Deans and canons are appointed supposedly because of their special gifts and experience, and so are their principal lay officers. It is not always easy to maintain a comradely spirit among a group of colleagues maybe of varied background, interests and opinions, appointed with an eye to equally diverse objectives. The performance of statutory duty alone does not guarantee harmony, and indeed may be itself a source of dissension when the responsibilities of one office holder conflict with the prerogatives of another. In a university college the size of the governing body can to a great extent absorb difference, and even conflict: it is less easy in a small capitular body. At York, moreover, the Dean formally was simply *primus inter pares*, and behind the

1. Adrian Leek, *op cit.*, p. 21.
2. Charles Smyth, *Cyril Forster Garbett*, 1959, p. 283.
3. *ibid.*, p. 339.
4. Friends *Report*, 1989, p. 16.
5. In a letter to the author.

Administrative Committee lay the ultimate authority of the prebendaries of the Regular Chapter. (Milner's pamphlet, *York Minster Its Care and Management* (n.d.) simply describes the formal position of the four dignitaries – Dean and three canons.)

Milner's will was strong; his characteristic tendency was 'to act rather as a single-minded and wholly benevolent autocrat'.[1] To some the autocracy was more evident than the benevolence. Furthermore, certain of Milner's principal interests coincided with those of colleagues. The Chancellor, Frederick Harrison, was not only Librarian, but was rightly held to be the leading authority on the York glass.[2] Canon George Addleshaw, the Treasurer (later Dean of Chester), was an authority on liturgy and architecture,[3] and in his official rôle had immediate responsibility for Minster finance. He was surprised to hear in 1960 that plans were afoot for a Nave organ console! And in 1952 Milner referred to 'my own special province, the handling of investments',[4] thus exposing an area of possible disagreement, or at least of unease. What one devotee of Milner described as his 'style of management' was unwelcome to some, amusing though it was to others. Yet, strangely, Milner failed decisively to intervene when there were problems – never resolved – arising from Minster Choir School regulations. Here was an area which needed firm leadership for the avoidance of friction.

Milner's contribution to the major development of the Minster Library has already been described. To that enterprise he brought enthusiasm, profound knowledge and personal generosity, including royalties from his own publications. It was fortunate that he was able to call in A. N. L. Munby from King's to advise on policy, and that he enjoyed the warm support of Canon Addleshaw on the importance of the Library in Minster schemes. The appointment of Canon Reginald Cant in 1957 as Chancellor and Librarian was a great boon: a scholar of distinction, eirenic, quietly determined to implement Munby's report, he also had the trust of Milner, and fostered the continuing progress of the Library in the years when the Dean's health began to fail. (In his last illness Milner changed his bedroom to gain a view of the building work on the Library.) Another fortunate circumstance was the stimulation of the Minster Library expansion consequent upon the planning of the University at York.

The inspiration for much of his efforts for the Library was Milner's love of books – which he expected to be beautiful as well as useful. A required source book used by mediaeval glaziers to design their windows was the *Legenda Aurea*, the Golden Legend, a manual consisting largely of the lives of the saints drawn up by Jacobus of Voragine[5] in the middle of the 13th century. Milner purchased the magnificent Kelmscott Press edition of the English translation, made and originally printed by William Caxton. Other important sources were the illumi-

---

1. J. M. Nicholson, *The King's School Magazine*, Summer, 1963, p. 3.
2. e.g. *The Painted Glass of York*, 1927; *Stained Glass of York Minster* (Studio Publications), n.d.
3. e.g. *The Architectural Setting of Anglican Worship*, 1948, with Frederick Etchells. The excellent pamphlet by Addleshaw on the *Five Sisters Window* (the Charles Dickens story with a description of the glass) was highly successful.
4. M-W Papers, I.1 (a note).   5. A Dominican; Archbishop of Genoa, 1292–1298.

nations in mediaeval liturgical manuscripts, and Milner secured the best books which reproduced and analysed them. Purchased in paper covers, he had them handsomely bound, advised by Douglas Cockerell, Director of the Fitzwilliam Museum. Gifts to the Library from 'Philologus' arose, of course, from genuine devotion to the cause, but were also a device to persuade the Chapter to allow the Dean, Treasurer and Librarian to purchase more books, with the promise that then further gifts would follow! Milner's impish humour can be detected in such beneficent plots.

One of his bookish interests was the purchase of detective novels, which he had read avidly in the Cambridge years. The copies bought between the wars filled a small upstairs room in the Deanery, and on his death they were passed as a collection to the J. B. Morrell Library of the University of York, and have subsequently been augmented.

Milner had the advantage of considerable private means. He inherited £40,000, but achieved a mastery of the stock market, learning at King's from John Maynard Keynes, and becoming 'more venturesome than his broker'.[1] Parsimonious in small matters, frugal in domestic affairs, he was a bountiful benefactor to those causes which were dear to his heart. His financial generosity was directed towards the institutions in which he could exercise a good measure of control and where his practical advice on policy was valued. Not all his gifts for the Minster were acclaimed, yet his fortunate financial position allowed him to purchase furniture and ornaments which he deemed worthy. 'I bought them on spec,' he wrote of two 16th century walnut stalls.[2] His considerable gifts for the King's School, Tynemouth, for example, were the outcome of his enthusiasm for his new Woodard school and his powerful rôle as Provost of the Northern Division of the Woodard Corporation. His financial acumen also entitled him to collect pots and pictures, several of which he gave away in his lifetime.

Nevertheless in his last year at York he complained to the Church Commissioners that the decanal stipend had remained at £2,000 a year since the 15th century 'without a rise'.[3] (This was the time when the salaries of deans and canons were being reviewed.) He declared that it cost him £500 a year more than his salary to meet the demands of office, which, he stated, were met through his private means.

In his *Who's Who* entry Milner gave 'Modern pottery, stained glass, rose growing', as his hobbies. There could have been listed several other interests, including the cultivation of heather (Latin *Erica*).[4] What is abundantly clear is that he never studied a subject superficially, be it lamp-posts or liturgies. He never dabbled. Thus, his knowledge of cricket scores was detailed: he had been a cricketer himself, and the 'faded Hampshire Hogs blazer [had] added tone to many a match between the Fellows and the Choir School', at King's.[5]

Where others presumed to offer opinions on which they were inade-

---

1. Patrick Wilkinson, *op cit.*, p. 29.
2. M-W Papers II, 8, 25 June 1962 (to Miss E. H. E. Senior).
3. M-W Papers VI, 13, 21 September 1962. The statement was inaccurate.
4. Was there a new variety designated *Erica Erica*, or is this a Milnerian myth?
5. Wilkinson, *op cit.*, p. 8.

Plate 2. Eric Milner-White surveying the scene. (Photograph: York Minster Library.)

quately informed, he could be sharp. To a firm of glass-makers who protested when the Minster glaziers had advertised their readiness to undertake work elsewhere he wrote dismissively:

'Your letter causes me considerable astonishment. The whole strength of the Minster Glass Workshop is two. But the work they do is, and always will be, scientifically antiquarian, a class of which your members are not trained or capable.'[1]

One important area in which Milner seemed to show little active interest was the fabric of the Minster itself. He claimed in the pamphlet on *York Minster Its Care and Management* that every square inch of stone had been examined.[2] But the impending danger to the structure, notably the central tower, was evidently not perceived. The appointment of Sir Bernard Feilden as architect under Dean Alan Richardson ushered in an era of major work, and it is perhaps significant that the appeal for the fabric earlier in Milner's time earned far less space in his annual reports than the accounts of both glass restoration and regular acquisitions and adornments. Nevertheless, that appeal had his wholehearted support. There was some discussion in the years 1958–9 on the supposed effects of vibration caused by traffic in Deangate (denied by the City Engineer), and on 8 January 1959 Milner wrote an article for the *Yorkshire Post*, 'Does York Minster matter?' A small Works Committee (the Dean, the Treasurer, Bishop Hubbard) set up a few years earlier seems to have had little effect on major matters affecting the fabric. Had it been suspected that there was a major threat to the building, the professional advisers would presumably have warned the Dean and Chapter.

One of the duties and privileges of deans is to extend hospitality. Milner's Visitors' Book, now in the King's Archives,[4] is a record of some interest, though, as single dates only are usually given, it is guesswork to discover who stayed overnight. Colleagues from King's came, among them Boris Ord, A. N. L. Munby, Provost Sheppard, and, shortly before Milner's death, his successor as Dean of King's, A. R. Graham-Campbell, by then Bishop of Colombo (at whose consecration in the Minster Milner had preached). Constant Lambert and Robert Helpmann were there in 1942 (the major interest in ballet was maintained at York); Lord Kilmaine (Pilgrim Trust) and Sir Keith Murray (University Grants Committee) were among what for a period of 22 years was numerically a modest number of guests, which included the significant visits of Sir Albert Richardson and Sir Ninian Comper. (Lord Beveridge's name also appears in the book.) The arrival of old King's students, some in Orders, were a delight to him, though godsons and, above all, members of his family, gave him the greatest joy. His nieces had unbounded affection for him.

He was very generous to his godsons, and he appeared at his most

---

1. M-W Papers II, 6, 22 August, 1961.
2. p. 10.
3. M-W Papers V, 4, esp. February, 1959.
4. C 20.

relaxed with children. Clearly his relationship with the young was most evident at King's, and old members of the Choir School express their admiration for his teaching there and for his Confirmation classes. (One of them reports that many regarded Milner as infallible.) At York there is evidence of his continuing enjoyment in the company of the young, especially in the schools with which he was associated.

York was in some important ways a very difficult setting for the exercise of Milner's gifts. Among his colleagues in the College he was respected, though it was recognized that he was something of a schemer. It was Milner himself who described his mind as 'devious'. ('What do you think are his *real* reasons?' is said to have been the remark of a (friendly) colleague after a Milnerian speech in a College meeting.) He was allowed his head in Chapel affairs, and in College matters he established a warm relationship with Sheppard, Keynes and others (among whom was George Rylands, for some time lay Dean, who speaks of Milner's 'fancy and imagination' in the College Council). When a plan was afoot to publish volumes on Memorials of the College he was, with Maynard Keynes, John Clapham and John Saltmarsh, appointed to the committee overseeing it, with special responsibility for the fourth volume on the history of the Chapel.[1]

With a minority of undergraduates he was a revered counsellor and friend. He had a deep and lifelong influence on many of them (not solely ordinands), and they recall, not only his spiritual guidance, but his enthusiastic encouragement of their interest in the arts – for instance, in the work of A. K. Nicholson, his favourite glass painter. (Throughout his life he was always on the lookout for new artists.) His ministry was very effective with the committed Christians: with the majority of undergraduates, however, he was a distant figure. The touch of extravagance, combined with shyness, the somewhat rarefied style in speech, not to mention the protracted silences at interviews, all were factors which for many inhibited *rapport*, even though few could have failed to recognise character of a singular order. Moreover, Milner was out of touch, academically, with the mainstream of University life, even in theology. The field of philosophical theology, for instance, was alien to him. Genuine intellectual difficulties had to be met on the enquirer's own ground, and that ground was unfamiliar.

York, with all its opportunities for the exercise of Milner's gifts, lacked the warmth of a Senior Combination Room community, and there was no substitute for those undergraduates among whom he had exercised a notable pastoral ministry. He always expressed admiration for tough Yorkshire qualities, but to the 'average' York citizen he appeared remote, even formidable. A cathedral is not usually a parish church also, and a dean has no formal pastoral responsibility other than that for employees whose welfare ought to be his concern. Pastoral work, as ordinarily understood, is exercised occasionally by the head

---

1.   Patrick Wilkinson and Christopher Morris, *John Saltmarsh*, 1975, p. 4.

of a Chapter, but such ministry tends to be fortuitous. To those who came to Milner as confessor he was a comfort and a valued guide. For those who learned from him artistic discrimination there is enduring gratitude (on that score 'my model Dean', writes a holder of that office elsewhere). His care for the choristers – inevitably less immediately evident than at King's – was genuine. It was characteristic of that care that he should offer a room at the Deanery for an ex-chorister to study in quiet as he prepared for his university entrance. Yet the somewhat grand manner, while unfailingly courteous, could – and did to some – give the impression of patronage. Milner's standards were those of the upper middle class, and perhaps he was old-fashioned even for his day (though we have yet to learn that a thing is wrong because it is old-fashioned). Among his principles was a deep respect for bishops as *numinous* figures with Apostolick authority (the 'k' as evident in speech as in writing). On the other hand *The Book of Hugh and Nancy* – mentioned elsewhere in this volume – embodies social attitudes which would widely be regarded as unacceptable (including the conde-scending, 'They do teach you well at the Council school').[1] Milner's interests in and devotion to schools could hardly have flourished in any but those of independent and Church foundation.

At St John's College, York,[2] he acted dutifully as Chairman of the governing body in the place of Archbishop Garbett, and was much appreciated for acquiescing in the shedding by the College of its Victor-ian 'charity' status and the consequent transfer of greater responsibility to governors and staff – a more professional affair. Again, courtesy was never wanting, but the evidence suggests that he failed fully to appreciate the Christian educational potential of the College, training, as it did, thousands of teachers at home and abroad. It was significant of his understanding of the pecking order of institutions that he expressed astonishment that the Provost of a cathedral should resign to become Principal of (another) *training college*. Given these social presuppo-sitions, could it be justifiably claimed that Milner was a snob? The answer to that question is an emphatic 'no'. Writing of B. K. Cunning-ham, Principal of Westcott House, 1919–1944, Bishop John Moorman recalled B.K.'s ideal of 'the English gentleman in Holy Orders,' and yet recorded, 'He was not in any sense of the term a "snob", for a snob will always alter his behaviour to suit the company in which he finds himself, and B.K. never did that'.[3] That observation applies appropri-ately to Milner.

For his family he had a deep love. In his 'Who's Who' entry he referred to his father, Sir Henry Milner-White, whom he revered. His mother died when he was six, and 'my dear Mother' of whom he often spoke was his Father's second wife. His younger brothers, Norman and Basil, died young. Their brother, Rudolph, had three daughters, whose

1. Written with Eleanor Duckett, 1939, p. 52.
2. Where Milner recommended Francis Howard Spear to design the windows in the (former) College Chapel.
3. John R. H. Moorman, *B. K. Cunningham, a Memoir*, 1947, p. 105.

company Uncle Eric greatly enjoyed (one of them a devoted god-daughter).

For friends there was evident affection (he subscribed himself 'Thine'). Notable among them was Gerald Fitzgerald (contemporary at Harrow and King's), who was killed in 1915, and (Bishop) Philip Loyd. Affection, however, was not easily communicated, though friendship endured, as did adverse judgements. Disapproval was unequivocal. The effects of insomnia, endured for so long after his War experiences, were known to few. He seemed to enjoy admiration, and it has to be acknowledged that some of his swans to others seemed geese. Yet moments of self-caricature were not lacking, the puffing and blowing magnified and the diction yet more precise. 'He was a Dean,' wrote one of his severest critics, 'take him for all in all, we shall not see his like again.' But Milner's mode of life and ministry could not possibly have been exercised in days when local and national committees have by law a voice and vote in Cathedral affairs. His prodigious range of activity required a style of 'management' no longer acceptable. But its successful application also needed exact knowledge and aesthetic sensitivity, and Milner had a remarkable combination of both. His judgement was not infallible and his method of management was circuitous, combined with a degree of naiveté, but the achievement for York was indisputable.

Whatever human failings Milner had, his genuine and wholehearted commitment was that of a priest who perceived God through the beauty of nature, the beauty of things created by man, the beauty of music, the beauty of words – and the beauty of silence.

Beauty in all its forms speaks an eternal voice.

Some major furnishings introduced under Dean Milner-White

Irvine Watson

Note: A description of furniture acquired was usually given by the Dean in the Friends Annual Reports. Attention is drawn here to 'Four Hundred Years. Architects, Sculptors, Painters, Craftsmen, 1560–1960, whose work is to be seen in York Minster', by G. W. O. Addleshaw, 1962 and 'Seven Hundred Years, The Furnishings and Fittings of York Minster from the 13th to the 20th Century', by Arthur G. Widdess (additions by John Toy), 1983. Some of the furnishings are not now (1991) in the positions for which they were designed, or have been substantially altered.

NAVE

Sword and mace rest: painted wood of the Queen Anne period. Transferred in 1942 from the (disused) church St John's Church, Micklegate, York.

Lectern platform and rail: the platform of oak, designed by Sir Albert Richardson and made by Robert Thompson of Kilburn in 1946. The 18th c. wrought-iron rail given by Colonel and Mrs Gardner, of Gray's Court, York. The two lights (18th c. Venetian), formerly at Welbeck Abbey, added in 1948.

Pulpit of dark oak, designed by Sir Ninian Comper. The memorial to Archbishop Lang and Archbishop Temple. Dedicated on 17 July 1948.

Seats for the choir and clergy: walnut, designed by Sir Albert Richardson, the choir seats made by Rattee and Kett, of Cambridge; the stalls for the dean and canons made by John P. White, of Bedford. Installed between 1948 and 1952. The gift and memorial of Lady Milner-White.

Altar rails: walnut, designed by Sir Albert Richardson. Made by Rattee and Kett. Given in 1950 by Mrs. A. N. Cooper and her family in memory of Canon Cooper, Vicar of Filey.

Suffragan bishop's chair: oak, designed by Sir Albert Richardson. Made by Robert Thompson, of Kilburn (1950). The memorial to Bishop H. St. J. S. Woollcombe.

Altar table: oak, in three sections. Designed by W. J. Green (Clerk of Works) and made by Robert Littlewood (Minster Stoneyard) (1955)

Archbishop's throne: guerea (an African mahogany), designed by Sir Albert Richardson and made by John P. White of Bedford. The memorial to Archbishop Garbett. Dedicated on 7 October 1959.

Plate 3. The Nave Pulpit by Sir Ninian Comper. (Photograph: Jim Kershaw, L.B.I.P.P., F.S.A.I.)

The Pater Noster Chapel (near the north-west door) The altar table (which had been in St Stephen's Chapel from 1937–45) designed by Sir Walter Tapper (Consulting Architect 1908–35). Made by R. Bridgeman and Sons, of Lichfield. The reredos (a painting of The Crucifixion, by Charles Ricketts R. A.) given by the Friends in 1948.
The chapel was completed in 1963 with the ironwork screen designed by Francis Johnson and made by W. Dowson, of Kirkbymoorside.

NORTH TRANSEPT

Astronomical clock: designed by Dr R.d'E. Atkinson, Chief Assistant, Royal Greenwich Observatory. Made in the Observatory workshop. The silver dials and sun track made by W. F. Knight, of Wellingborough. The bronze frieze of seraphs made by Maurice Lambert R. A, sculptor, of London. The case and hanging cross designed by Sir Albert Richardson. Decoration of the Ball of Earth and of the spandrels on the east and west faces by H. J. Stammers, of York. The memorial to the airmen of Britain, the Commonwealth and five allied nations who operated from stations in Yorkshire, Durham and Northumberland and died in the 1939–45 War. Unveiled by H. R. H. The Duke of Edinburgh on 1 November 1955.

CHOIR

Chantry of God's Will (1949). Over the monument of Archbishop Savage (1501–07). Designed by Sir Albert Richardson. Made by Robert Thompson, of Kilburn. A memorial to three successive Registrars of the Province and Diocese, William Hudson (1797–1864), Henry Arthur Hudson (1841–1911) and Arthur Vaughan Hudson (1869–1940), grandfather, father and son.
Gospel ambo (1952); designed by Sir Albert Richardson. Memorial to Squadron Leader K. T. P. Terry D.F.C. (d. 1944).
High Altar rails: (1952) designed by Sir Albert Richardson. Made by John P. White, of Bedford.

LADY CHAPEL

Return stalls and kneeling desks (1945): designed by Sir Charles Peers (Consulting Architect 1935–46). Made by Robert Thompson, of Kilburn. Given by Miss Amy Clark.

CRYPT

Font and cover: the font (15th c.) moved in 1942 from the disused Bedern Chapel and placed within the well-head on the traditional site of King Edwin's baptism by Paulinus in 627. The cover designed by Sir Ninian Comper. Made by Rattee and Kett, of Cambridge. The figures painted by W. J. Butchart, of West Croydon.

Side altars; (1942) Rebuilt on the original footpaces, one in Tadcaster and the other in Huddlestone stone. Dedicated to St Edwin (north) and St Hilda (south).

Notes

C. G. Lang, Archbishop of York 1909–28.
W. Temple, Archbishop of York 1929–42.
C. F. Garbett, Archbishop of York 1942–55.
H. St. J. S. Woolcombe, Bishop of Whitby 1923–9, of Selby 1939–40.
Sir Albert Richardson, 1880–1964, Consulting Architect to the Dean and Chapter, 1946–64; President of the Royal Academy, 1954–6.
Sir Ninian Comper, 1864–1960; taught by C. E. Kempe, and articled to G. F. Bodley and T. Garner.

Childhood Memories of Eric Milner-White

Mary Holtby

In 1940 there appeared a revised version of *The Cuddesdon Office Book*, edited by Eric Milner-White; three years earlier, in collaboration with Eleanor S. Duckett, an American, he had published a novel, *The Book of Hugh and Nancy*. As a child I was involved with the compiling of the one and the contents of the other.

When my father, Eric Graham, was Principal of Cuddesdon, the various activities of the college ensured a constant flow of visitors through our house. Amongst these was 'Milner', then Dean of King's and famously responsible for the large number of ordinands who passed from the one establishment to the other (incidentally providing the influences which persuaded two of my brothers to depart from the Oxford tradition of their parents). Described in the Preface to the Office Book as 'the old student whose liturgical skill and diligent care' made it what it was, he regularly visited and corresponded with my father during the pre-war years.

So Milner was a familiar figure in our household in the '30s, and, as it happened, his niece Lalage and I were at the same boarding-school, though as she was two years older than I and had, even so, come into the school two years later, I didn't know her very well – and her uncle's offer in 1938 of the post of Maid of Honour to her as Queen of the King's Choristers' camp at Batcombe came as a complete surprise. This is where *The Book of Hugh and Nancy* comes in, with its barely fictionalized account of the set-up and the characters and activities concerned with it – the exact nature of which (I hadn't then heard of the book) I found difficult to grasp beforehand, but into which I entered with total enthusiasm when we arrived. As his niece has remarked since, Milner's 'love of make-believe and ritual overlapped and had full play and we all put in our bit', taking our parts in the 'Royal' household where, punctuated with suitable ceremonial, the Queen and her court (a rigid hierarchy of choristers and ex-choristers, ordinands and chaplain, each rank with its appropriate title) enjoyed expeditions all over Somerset, crazy sporting events on the local fields and hills, camp-fires with traditional songs and evening prayers. The organizer and moving spirit was, of course, the 'Archbishop', Milner himself, who survives in my battered photograph album wearing shorts and a superb panama,

Plates 4 and 5. King's Choristers' camp at Batcombe. (Photographs: Mary Holtby.)

talking to a group of boys, drinking tea, swiping with manic energy at a rounders ball . . .

My new knowledge of him began with the drive to Batcombe in his small black car, 'Canticles' ('She is black, but comely', he explained). I was desperately shy, but when we stopped at Avebury Ring I couldn't fail to share his enthusiasm, communicated in a way which was to be demonstrated repeatedly in subsequent outings with the campers. I recall churches and great houses, sites of historic importance and wonderful places for picnics, ceremonial 'colonization' in the name of the Queen of special spots in the Somerset countryside. I don't know what the older, more sophisticated members of the party felt about it all, but they certainly played up, and the young loved it.

The invitation was repeated the following year (1939); this time I shared my duties as Maid of Honour with the sister of an old chorister, and though I enjoyed it all enormously (and fell in love a second time), some slight shadow must have hung over our proceedings. That this would be the last of such holidays must have been evident to the elders, though I have to confess that I clearly remember responding with indignation and disbelief when my own family commented on the fact when I returned home. I had no idea of the imminence of war, nor that the Batcombe camps would acquire a symbolic significance in my life as the end of childhood.

It was in effect the end of my relationship with Milner, too. Though I saw him occasionally in later life and he was always amiable, there was the slight awkwardness which frequently attends a meeting with a child-friend (and he was wonderful with children) who has now grown up – a process which in some respects was, I believe, distasteful to him, though, in the words of his niece, 'there was enough of the teacher in him to relish the flowering of pupils and protégés'. To me he remains an integral part of a particularly happy period in my life; and I think he would be pleased that I learned the names of Kempe and Webb when church-crawling with him in Somerset – and remembered them.

The Dean as Collector

Sarah Riddick, former Art Assistant, York City Art Gallery

Eric Milner-White was a man with a highly developed aesthetic sense who bought works of art extensively throughout his life. He derived great pleasure from looking at and understanding them, and could not resist enriching his surroundings with choice examples. He bought not only for himself but for several public institutions: the Fitzwilliam Museum in Cambridge, York Minster and York City Art Gallery being the prime beneficiaries. His taste and expertise ranged widely from Persian rugs and metal work to pictures and modern ceramics. To all these areas he applied a basic collecting philosophy: the object must be loved profoundly, only buy the very best, and the money will come from somewhere.[1] Following these principles, he made notable purchases particularly of modern pottery and to a lesser extent pictures. It is the aim of this chapter to reveal the scope and significance of the Dean's collecting in these two areas.

From around 1914 until the mid–1950s, Dean Milner-White purchased at least fifty-six pictures.[2] According to Hans Hess, Curator of York City Art Gallery from 1947 until 1967, the Dean bought:

> paintings of the period of his own youth, the works of artists which were truly modern when he himself was young. ... Whistler and Sickert, Conder, Tonks and Wilson Steer were his favourites. He preferred small, intimate pictures with which he could live in a happy serenity of enjoyment.[3]

James Abbott McNeill Whistler (1834–1903) was probably the most influential artist working in England in his day and was a firm favourite of the Dean, who bought four paintings which at the time were attributed to this artist:

Portrait Study of a Man (Fitzwilliam Museum, Cambridge, PD. 29–1970)
Symphony in Grey and Brown: Lindsey Row, Chelsea (Fitzwilliam Museum, Cambridge, PD. 17–1948)
Woman Sewing (Fitzwilliam Museum, Cambridge, PD. 975–1963)
Nocturne in Blue and Gold (York City Art Gallery, 1028)

Only the first of these however, *Portrait Study of a Man*, is now still attributed to Whistler. The second and third pictures are believed to

---

1. Information supplied verbally be the Reverend John McMullen.
2. Fifty-six pictures are known to the author, more may well exist.
3. Hans Hess, 'Editorial', *Preview*, XVI, no. 63, July 1963, p. 594.

be imitations and the fourth has been reattributed to Walter Greaves (1846–1930). Dean Milner-White had already bought a painting by Walter Greaves in 1948, *Japanese Figures on Chelsea Embankment*, which he presented to York City Art Gallery in the same year.

After Whistler, Dean Milner-White particularly liked the work of Walter Richard Sickert (1860–1942) and is known to have purchased five pictures by this artist:

The Butcher's Shop (York City Art Gallery, 591)
The Piazzetta, Venice (York City Art Gallery, 1029)
La Rue de la Boucherie with the Church of St Jacques, Dieppe (York City Art Gallery, 1044)
Church of St Jacques, Dieppe (Fitzwilliam Museum, Cambridge, PD. 28–1970)
The Visitor (York City Art Gallery, 924)[1]

He purchased other examples of works by the Camden Town Group (of which Sickert was the leading light): two oils by Harold Gilman (1876–1919), *The Artist's Daughters* (York City Art Gallery, 209), of which he is said to have been very fond, and *Interior with Nude* (York City Art Gallery, 725), about which the Reverend John McMullen remembers him as having been rather coy! One of his earliest purchases was Spencer Frederick Gore's *From a Canal Bridge, Chalk Farm Road*, bought from Mrs Gore in 1914 or 1915. He sold this painting, only to buy it back again in 1952, and finally to present it to York City Art Gallery in 1963.

The Dean is known to have bought three works by Philip Wilson Steer (1860–1942), the evocative landscape painter. These were: *Boats on the Beach, Southwold* (York City Art Gallery, 919), c. 1888–89; *Dover Coast* (York City Art Gallery, 1027), c. 1918; and *Kimono* (York City Art Gallery, 1032), c. 1894. He also bought one painting each by Charles Conder (1868–1909), the landscape and decorative painter, and Henry Tonks (1862–1937), the influential teacher; these were: *Yport* (York City Art Gallery, 1030) and *The Toilet* (York City Art Gallery, 1026) of 1892 and 1896 respectively.

While at Cambridge, Dean Milner-White had become friendly with Roger Fry (1866–1934)[2] who from 1910 was recognized as the most influential art critic of his time in England. Through Fry he met all the Bloomsbury Group and so had access to one of the most avant-garde circles of his day. While no doubt finding this milieu stimulating, it did not cause him to buy Bloomsbury paintings; his taste in paintings was predominantly for those which exhibited modern French influence. Fry was responsible for making modern French painting widely known in England through the two Post-Impressionist exhibitions he organized at the Grafton Galleries, London, in 1910 and 1912. Before this time the work of Van Gogh, Gauguin, Cézanne, Matisse and Picasso was largely unknown in England. Dean Milner-White did not buy the

1. *The Visitor* has been recently reattributed to Anna Hope (Nan) Hudson (1869–1957) by Dr Wendy Baron.
2. Information supplied verbally by the Reverend John McMullen.

work of these giants, except for one Gauguin, *Landscape* of 1873, bought for presentation to the Fitzwilliam Museum in 1952. He did however buy two oils by Camille Pissarro (1830–1903), *Route de Port-Marly* painted between 1860 and 1867, and *Effet de Neige, Eragny* of 1895, both now in the Fitzwilliam Museum.

Other picture collectors of the time bought modern French pictures. From 1922 Samuel Courtauld had started to build the magnificent collection of Impressionist paintings which he gave to the Courtauld Institute of Art. The Contemporary Art Society presented the Tate with its first Gauguin in 1917, and Michael Sadler bought four Gauguins in Paris in 1911. Lord Duveen, the dealer, presented the Tate with its first Degas in 1916, and a Gauguin in 1919.

Nor did Dean Milner-White collect the most important contemporary British painters, such as Barbara Hepworth, Henry Moore, Ben Nicholson and Victor Pasmore. He seems to have patronized very few truly contemporary painters and the only one who stands out is John Piper (born in 1903). He greatly admired Piper's work and apparently predicted that he would become a glass designer,[1] an unusual route for an artist, but one which Piper did in fact follow.

While Dean Milner-White was buying pictures, certainly from 1915 onwards, he bought the majority of his pictures in the first half of the 1950s. This may have been primarily for financial reasons. Although he was left about £40,000 by his father in 1922,[2] he did not inherit his full share of his father's estate until his step-mother died in 1951. By this time it seems likely that he had significantly increased his capital through shrewd investments. He had befriended Maynard Keynes, the economist at King's College, Cambridge, and gleaned much about finance from him.

Dean Milner-White's picture collection consisted of a group of unpretentious pictures, in the main well-chosen, bought to adorn the walls of their discerning owner. A note in his handwriting headed *Pictures to York Art Gallery* lists pictures hanging in specific rooms at the Deanery in York.[3] For instance the Henry Tonks is listed as being in the dining room, and is remembered by the Reverend John McMullen as hanging over the fireplace. Other pictures in this room include Wilson Steer's *Dover Coast*, Sickert's *The Piazzetta, Venice*, Conder's *Yport* and the two paintings by John Armstrong (1893–1973), *Funeral of a Poet* and *Goatherd*. The 'Whistler' *Nocturne in Blue and Gold* now attributed to Walter Greaves, was also listed as hanging in this room, although Mr. McMullen remembers it hanging in the Dean's bedroom. The hall boasted what the Dean refers to as Wilson Steer's 'Single Figure', presumably *Kimono*, Emile Bouneau's *Boy in a Red Shirt*, and Sir Stanley Spencer's *The Deposition and Rolling Away of the Stone*. Ker-Xavier Roussel's *Silenus* was to be found in the drawing

---

1. Ibid.
2. Patrick Wilkinson, *Eric Milner-White, 1884–1963*, King's College, Cambridge, 1963, p. 29.
3. See Milner-White file at York City Art Gallery.

Plate 6. *Interior with Nude* by Harold Gilman. (Photograph: York City Art Gallery.)

room and Spencer Gore's *From a Canal bridge, Chalk Farm Road*, was in the study.

Dean Milner-White's picture collecting was essentially fluid. He rarely kept pictures for more than a few years. Most interestingly, many pictures were bought not for himself but for immediate presentation to museums, in the first place for the Fitzwilliam Museum, and later for York City Art Gallery. In fact many of the pictures which are considered his best were bought for one or other of these museums. Both Gustave Courbet's *The Glade*, and Gwen John's *The Convalescent* were bought and presented to the Fitzwilliam in 1951, while Paul Gauguin's *Landscape* was presented in the following year and Harold Gilman's *Interior with Nude* was bought and presented to York in 1955. Other pictures were kept for only a few years before being passed to museums, pictures such as Gwen John's *Young Woman in a Red Shawl* purchased in 1952 and presented to York in 1956, and Nan Hudson's *The Visitor* purchased as by Sickert in 1954, and presented in 1958.

Perhaps it is not surprising that the Dean should have collected pictures at all. Anyone alive to the beauties of art will want to adorn his or her walls. What was much more unusual was that he should have collected ceramics, and a type of ceramic almost unknown at the time.

From 1925 until 1962, Dean Milner-White made an outstanding collection of what is today known as pioneer studio pottery. The pots were made in the 20th century (apart from two 19th century pieces of Martinware) and most were bought by the Dean during the 1920s and 1930s. Comprising around three hundred pots from the work of some thirty potters, the collection is particularly important for the work of three potters: William Staite Murray, Bernard Leach and Shoji Hamada. Indeed, the Milner-White collection contains the most important collection of Staite Murray pots in the world, some of the most famous Leach pots and the best group of Hamada pots outside Japan.

The Dean's awareness of modern pottery started in 1925. He was in New Bond Street when he stumbled across an exhibition of pots by Reginald Wells (1877–1951) at the Fine Art Society. He was completely overwhelmed by what he saw and in his own words:

It was by pure chance c. 1925. I walked into a Bond St. Gallery & saw a show of stoneware pots by Reg. Wells. Transfixed. Sat there 2 hours – forgot lunch! At the end, I bought (£20) A stranger, seeing my interest, said that in another gallery in Bond St was an exhibition of pots by an artist-craftsman of whom he thought even more highly. I went there . . . picking up . . . Murray.[1]

This day started the lifelong interest which was to culminate in the finest collection of pioneer studio pottery formed by an individual in the first half of this century. The Dean instinctively knew that he

1. See Milner-White's MS, notes, undated, at York City Art Gallery.

had come across something special and was determined to make a representative collection:

I knew I had come across something not only good, but *v. good*. I found an aesthetic delight, a thrill, over a fine pot which no other branch of art had ever been able to give me . . . and worked hours, days, weeks, correcting Certificate Papers in History from schools all over England, to get the money to buy. I bought only the best. How I beat my foes![1]

His collecting of modern pots was particularly unusual because they were so little known at the time. The prevailing taste in ceramics was for fine porcelain made by factories such as Chelsea, Derby, Spode and Worcester, a taste which had developed in the 18th century with the importation of Ming porcelain from the East.

A tradition of hand-made pottery had survived in England despite the increasing predominance of factory ware. By the 20th century, however, comparatively few people bought hand-made pottery. The major impetus for a revival of interest in hand-made pottery came from the East through the discovery of ancient Chinese ceramics mainly from the Sung dynasty (960–1279). These wares came to light due to the building of the Chinese railways at the turn of the century. During construction, numerous ancient tombs were uncovered which contained great quantities of ceramics from this earlier period. These pots, made from stoneware rather than porcelain, were of a completely different character from the later Ming wares. Though often technically imperfect, their forms were spontaneous productions of personal creativity and were covered with extraordinarily rich and exciting glaze effects. Soon examples started to find their way to Great Britain, but it was not until 1910 when the Burlington Fine Arts club held an exhibition of early Chinese pottery and porcelain that this ware became widely known. From this time many artists and amateurs started to become interested in making pottery.

These early 'studio' potters struggled to survive. There was little technical information published and they had to learn by trial and error. It all took an immense amount of determination and effort to succeed. Most of the potters lived very simply, and only just managed to keep going.

There were few serious collectors of pots in the early decades of this century. Dean Milner-White described the narrow circle of interest in studio pottery thus:

The people interested in the work of Wells, Murray, Leach during [the] '20s cd be counted on [the] finger[s] of one hand – Eumorphopoulos Marriott [the] A-C of the Times, Bernard Rackham, head of the department of Ceramics at the V & A. & that young & poor & unknown clergyman which was myself![2]

1. Ibid.
2. Ibid.

Patrons like Eric Milner-White were of enormous importance to these pioneers. William Staite Murray wrote to Milner-White:

I am no less grateful to you for buying my work, than you are to me in giving you pleasure by the beauty I create, for without buyers my work as a Potter would cease.[1]

The Dean was a loyal patron once he had become convinced of the worth of a potter. In his eyes Murray was the most original of the pioneers and he was determined to own outstanding examples of his work. Over 34 years he purchased 98 examples of Murray's work alone, costing him nearly £1,700.

He also gave valuable moral support to the potters, by writing to them and praising their work. From the replies that survive it is obvious this provided enormous encouragement. Charles Vyse wrote:

I am very grateful to you for your letter & appreciation. So very few have understood our attempt to break away in a new direction, & it is heartening to feel that you are in sympathy with it.[2]

Dean Milner-White was no mere acquisitor. He was, as has already been mentioned, a passionate and discriminating collector. He had a clear aesthetic philosophy, which was set out in the pamphlet accompanying the exhibition of his collection at York City Art Gallery in 1952. He purchased pots made only in stoneware, which he considered to be the aristocrat of ceramics. He looked for form, decoration and texture in a pot. This aesthetic is predominantly derived from Oriental ceramics. In that, he was a man of his time. He could have bought the work of Dame Lucie Rie (born 1902) and Hans Coper (1920–1981) – two of the most highly regarded potters working in the later years of his life – but he did not. Their work is in a very different style from the pieces represented in his collection.

The Dean's pots seem to have been bought much more for his own pleasure than were the paintings. He probably enjoyed having discovered something entirely new and greatly enjoyed the tactile qualities of pots; a number of people remember him picking up and caressing a pot as he talked to them in the Deanery. His favourite pot was reputed to have been Bernard Leach's magnificent vase 'Leaping Salmon' made in 1931. The Dean certainly enjoyed surrounding himself with the pots, as witnessed by two paintings of his sitting room at King's College, Cambridge by Harry Hicken.[3] These pictures show pots crowding every surface; his rooms must have been a nightmare to clean and visit. Several pots met with accidents.

Although the vast majority of the Dean's pots were bought for his own personal collection, he occasionally gave one away, perhaps as a friendly gesture to a fellow connoisseur, like a Leach jar he gave to George Wingfield Digby,[4] or as a wedding present.[5] He may have used

1. Letter from Staite Murray to Milner-White, 19 December 1928, at York City Art Gallery.
2. Letter from Charles Vyse to Milner-White, 6 March 1935, at York City Art Gallery.
3. The present whereabouts of these pictures is unknown.
4. Letter from George Wingfield Digby to Milner-White, 7 August 1950, at York City Art Gallery.
5. See Milner-White's General Catalogue, page headed 1956, at York City Art Gallery.

Plate 7. *Water Birds* by William Staite Murray.
(Photograph: York City Art Gallery.)

Plate 8. *Leaping Salmon* by Bernard Leach.
(Photograph: York City Art Gallery.)

gifts as a way of weeding his collection of pots which he no longer considered good, and he certainly used them as an attempt to stimulate or nurture an appreciation of modern pottery in others. In a letter to the Dean of 1933 Arden Constant, a young cleric, wrote:

Dearest Arch,
I went to see Vyse's exhibition in London on my way home, as you advised. It was a very pleasant shock. How slow I have been in appreciating his work! His glazes – remarkable! . . . I have come home to look at my two Vyses both of which you have given me. I am very fond of the bowl with octopus decorations.[1]

It is also possible that he had terrible tussles with his conscience between his desire to purchase and enjoy, and a religious belief that it was wrong to be acquisitive. Whatever the case, he gave away the first sizable number of pots to help establish Southampton Art Gallery in 1939. Southampton was his home town, and he gave a representative group of 47 in memory of his father. His major problem was what to do with the lion's share of his collection which he kept at home in the Deanery in York. Towards the end of his life, when he became ill from the cancer that would eventually kill him, he began to think seriously about the placement of his collection. Originally he wanted to leave it to the Fitzwilliam Museum in Cambridge; however the Syndics were only willing to accept the best 25 pots, and only then if no other museum was willing to take the collection. At this time Hans Hess was building the collections and reputation of York City Art Gallery. Dean Milner-White served on the Art Gallery Committee and was greatly in sympathy with Hess's objectives. He placed part of the collection on exhibition at the Art Gallery in 1952, and then decided to leave the whole collection to York. It was accepted with thanks.

For a full account of Dean Milner-White's pottery collection *see* Sarah Riddick, *Pioneer Studio Pottery: The Milner-White Collection* (Lund Humphries, London, in association with York City Art Gallery).

---

1. This letter is at York City Art Gallery. 'Arch' (for Archbishop) was the form of address adopted at the (King's) Choir School camps.

Textiles 1941–1963

Elizabeth Ingram

During Dean Milner-White's tenure of office, his love and appreciation of fine embroideries and other textiles was perhaps a minor, yet important facet of his adornment of the interior of the Minster. New fabrics were almost unobtainable during wartime and for some years afterwards and they also required clothing coupons. Antique fabrics were not limited by this restriction, and they could be bought at a reasonable price. Although it would have been in the knowledge that some ancient textiles would have a limited life because of their age, they did fulfill a useful and decorative purpose for some decades.

Not only did the Dean dig deep into his own pocket, but he encouraged the Friends of the Minster to sponsor many of his purchases, and also had the happy knack of encouraging benefactors to donate special textiles which had already caught his eye.

The Pater Noster chapel was first established at the West end of the Nave in 1945. The fine altar frontal of Italian appliqué-work mounted on blue silk, *c* 1620–30, together with the appliqué-work on the frame of the reredos picture above, are the oldest textiles in regular use in the Minster.

The Archbishop's throne in the Nave is hung with panels of late 17th century Italian velvet, while in the North Transept there is a fine dossal in St John's chapel. This mid–18th century French silk is hand-embroidered in a chinoiserie design, and was originally made up into a magnificent ball dress. The King's Own Yorkshire Light Infantry (whose chapel this is) purchased the dress in 1947, no doubt on the recommendation of the Dean, and had the very full skirt together with some additional silk turned into the dossal, where it adds a subtle touch of distinction to the sanctuary.

At the East end of the Minster, the altar in St Stephen's Chapel is dressed with a frontal made from two pieces of mid–18th century Chinese silk hand embroidered with flower sprays, bought in 1946.

From 1943–1968 the Lady Chapel altar was against the East wall and the frontal, dossal and riddel curtains were of fine 17th century Jacobean crewel-work, originally three pairs of bed curtains.

What is known as the Annunciation banner was brought to the notice of a potential benefactor in 1956. This true woven[1] tapestry has

---

1. True woven tapestry is a woven fabric made by passing coloured threads among fixed warp threads. The term is frequently misused to refer to embroidery work on canvas.

as its centrepiece a late 17th century panel depicting the Virgin with the Archangel Gabriel, and this is surrounded by other strips of woven tapestry to increase its size. On the back of the banner is recorded 'Remember before God the donor of this banner, Colonel William Henton Carver, DL, MP, JP, 1868–1961; tireless servant of God and his church, of his country and his fellow men'.

A second tapestry banner, woven as a bed cover in rural Norway c. 1685, is divided into four panels, recalling the visit of the Three Wise Men, here depicted as three crowned princes of Norwegian mediaeval art. It is a rare piece and was purchased in 1956.

St Hilda's banner, originally made by the Wantage Sisters to the design of Sir Ninian Comper for use at the Church Congress held in Middlesbrough in 1912, was hung in the crypt from 1945 to 1979, where it formed the reredos to St Hilda's altar. The hangings over the other two altars, which were installed in 1943, were a splendid late 15th century Crucifixion, probably North German, and showing the cross as the green branches of a tree and not as cut timber. The second embroidered panel, of the Virgin and child standing on a crescent moon which pierces the disc of the sun, is an allusion to the Virgin as Queen of Heaven. This second panel was mounted against a length of crimson cut velvet reputed to have come from the walls of a room at Holyrood Palace. St Hilda's banner reverted to use as a banner in 1979 but the two 15th century panels were removed at this time. The three frontals in the crypt were made up from a silk sari, a length of antique crimson velvet and an old red and gold damask woven for the coronation of Edward VII.

Another embroidery bought in 1954, but no longer in the Minster, was a Spanish altar frontal, c. 1530, framed by Dean Milner-White and hung in the South Choir aisle. Deterioration due to bright sunlight caused this piece to be removed in 1978 for eventual conservation. This frontal shows a representation of the Last Supper with the donors of the frontal kneeling to left and right of the table.

Before the Zouche chapel was reordered in 1977, the altar was dressed with a frontal and superfrontal of 18th century brocade, flanked by dossal and riddel curtains, said to have been woven in 1880 for the Princess of Wales (later Queen Alexandra).

It is not known if there were any hangings in the Choir pulpit and Archbishop's throne prior to the 1940's, but lengths of velvet were purchased in 1948 to line the pulpit. At the time it was thought to be original Spitalfields silk woven for Queen Anne in 1714, but subsequent research revealed that it was 19th century based on the original, though still an impressive fabric. Two red velvet dalmatics worked in silver thread, sent over to England from Russia, were purchased in 1943 and turned into the hangings for the Archbishop's throne. Marks are still visible where orphreys have been unpicked.

Plate 9.   The Norwegian Banner. (Photograph: Jim Kershaw, L.B.I.P.P., F.S.A.I.)

The stalls in the Choir sanctuary were hung with fragments of 18th century velvet and brocade, all removed in 1990 in a ragged state, but the adjacent Savage chantry is still furnished with striped blue and buff velvet, *c.* 1670.

The Dean was equally concerned with vestments, and both High and Low Mass sets were acquired, usually from Messrs Watts & Co., but some were made up by them and the Sisters of Bethany from old materials provided by the Dean. A beautiful early 18th century chasuble was given to the Minster in 1942 and an equally splendid Portuguese chasuble of the mid–18th century was bought by the Dean in 1957, together with four or five other 18th century pieces.

An amusing story is recorded in the Dean's letter in the 1947 Annual Report of the Friends. He had been captivated by two pieces of Chinese silk which HM Queen Mary had loaned for display at the Royal School of Needlework. The Dean wrote to the Queen and asked if he might have the pieces of silk for use in York Minister. Her Majesty graciously consented to this request, provided that the sum of £5 per piece be given to the Royal Naval Benevolent Trust. After this proviso had been carried out, the silk was made up into two burses and two veils. It transpired that the material consisted of fragments left over from a length of Chinese silk which the Emperor of China had given to Queen Victoria as a wedding present in 1837. The Dean was able to find a further length of silk woven to the same design, but in the 20th century, and from this he had made a chasuble and stole so that a Low Mass set was achieved. Many other small fragments of textiles were purchased over the years to be made up into altar cushions, burses, sets of apparel and book marks.

In 1943, the Dean, for the Dean and Chapter, received a most generous gift of vestments from the Rev. Edward George Forse, Vicar of St Katharine's Church, Southbourne, Bournemouth, from 1911 to 1935. The gift consisted of no less than nine Low Mass sets, all made by the St Katharine's Embroidery Guild under the direct supervision of Father Forse. In addition there were a dozen or more embroidered or lace-covered palls and four splendid albs. The Dean considered that these ornate, lace-encrusted albs were too High Church for the Minster and passed them on to a parish near York. Eight of the Low Mass sets survive, and many of the palls.

The Dean's generosity and forethought during his lifetime was extended by his will in which he bequeathed to the Minster a most impressive and valuable collection of Persian rugs, which are still to be seen in various chapels and especially in the Choir sanctuary.

The fine collection of antique embroideries, textiles, vestments and rugs in the Minster today, owes a great deal to Dean Eric Milner-White's good taste and enthusiasm over nearly a quarter of a century.

A Treasure House of Stained Glass

Peter Gibson, Superintendent, The York Glaziers Trust

York Minster contains the largest accumulated collection of mediaeval stained glass in England. In the 128 windows is every period of glass painting from the 12th century to the present day, a total of approximately two million separate pieces of glass. At the outbreak of the 1939–1945 war 80 of the most important windows in the Minster were removed for safety – a task which was to take more than two years to complete. Significantly, what was not removed was the glass of the Rose Window and that of the 14 Nave Clerestory windows.

When the Dean arrived at York most of the important glass was either not to be seen or was still being removed for war safety. Because he could not wait for the war to be over he arranged in 1944 that some panels of mediaeval glass belonging to the Great East Window should be brought out of storage to the glaziers' workshop for his inspection. He was more than disappointed that the panels, instead of depicting their scenes or figures as originally painted, were in a very misordered state. This presented a challenge that he relished, and he began instructing the two glaziers on the rearrangement of the mediaeval glass in order to recreate the original scenes or figures, and he continued to do this for the next 18 years in the glaziers' workshop.

The post-war restoration of the Minster glass under the direction of the Dean was one of the most exciting and fruitful periods in the history of the Cathedral. I count myself indeed more than fortunate to have had a close association with the glass during this unforgettable era.

Who could have wished for more than to be working for the enrichment of one of the greatest Cathedrals in the world, to be serving as an apprentice/craftsman on one of the finest collections of stained glass in the world, under the tuition of one of the most noted stained glass experts in the world!

The early days of my apprenticeship were exciting times with the Dean coming into the workshop almost daily and on some occasions two or even three times a day. He would also come into the workshop in the evenings and often on returning to the bench next morning I would find a note waiting on the panel I was working on suggesting some alteration or improvement to it.

The small team of Oswald Lazenby, Herbert Nowland and myself had one characteristic in common with the Dean concerning the re-arrangement of ancient glass – we all seemed to be 'tuned in' to the same wavelength as far as the way particular pieces of glass should be reordered. The Dean was always prepared to listen to any suggestions that were made and no decision by the Dean was ever taken hastily. If there was a particular problem with the panel that could not be readily resolved then the panel was put on one side so that we could all reflect on it and come up with ideas.

DEFENCE OF THE CRAFT

The Dean's acitivities in the world of stained glass were far from parochial. His advice was sought from far and wide, and many stained glass artists both known and unknown were indebted to him for his advice and words of encouragement and, one must not forget, also discouragement (although the Dean always referred to it as 'construc-tive criticism'). He never lost an opportunity to promote the art and craft of stained glass which he so dearly loved or to defend it, as he did on one particular occasion demonstrates. On 10 July 1956, at the Building Centre of London, an exhibition of contemporary stained glass was organized by the British Society of Master Glass Painters (of which the Dean was one of the Vice-Presidents) and the Worshipful Company of Glaziers and Painters on Glass, opened by Her Royal Highness the Duchess of Kent. I give below an extract from his speech:

'Stained glass is an art, whether major or minor depends on itself, first in so far as it understands and fulfils its function. And that is, to be a decoration to architecture. It is a subordinate art – and need not be ashamed of that; for it directly serves the mistress art, architecture; just as in history sculpture, admittedly a major art, has again and again been at its greatest when subordinately serving architecture.

And secondly, it can only be an art in so far as in its own creations it understands its material. It is NOT a canvas art or anything like it. It is NOT a sculptural art or anything like it.

It is a MOSAIC art. It paints (if we may use that word; there is none other) not with a brush but with fragments of coloured glass. Its privilege and power is to paint on light itself; being thereby not only the most brilliant art of colour known to man, but infinitely various as the light changes with each moment of every day, with every shift of the cloud and every burst of sun.

For these two reasons its subordination to its frame of stone and the luminousness of, so to speak, its bricks, stained glass is and must be a DECORATIVE art, wholly decorative, NOT realistic, NOT illustrative; an art in two dimensions; recession and perspective; motion, especially arrested motion, are out of place except within the narrowest decorative limits; they make nonsense of the grand and static frame. No art is the weaker for observing its proper disciplines.

The good glass artists of today, and they are not so few, have got beyond the idea of the later 19th century, that a window should illustrate for purposes of edification some Gospel or sacred scene. That generally meant a Sunday School picture executed with unsuitable materials and set incongrously in an architectural opening. Alas, as all glass-painters know, that it is still the first idea and demand of most donors who wish to commission a window. But this sort of sentimental mistake is dying, and the Church itself through its Diocesan Advisory Committees has done much to kill it and set the artist free.'

CRITICS

So it was that, one by one, as the windows were brought back from their war-time storage locations throughout Yorkshire, attempts were made by the small team headed by the Dean to rectify the misordering of the glass that had occurred over the centuries. The oversight of the workshop was in the experienced and capable hands of Mr Jesse Green, the Clerk of Works, and he, together with the Dean, planned the sequence of the return of the windows. Critics of the Dean's achievements on the Minster glass never gave him credit for his immense knowledge about stained glass of all ages. I would go even further and say that it was only because of the belief in his own knowledge of the history of glass painting and the technical skills allied to the crafts that he embarked on that great post-war task. If he had not considered himself up to the magnitude of the task he would not have started it.

ILLNESS OF THE DEAN

It was in the late 1950's that the Dean's health began to deteriorate, which was a great sadness to the workshop team. Nevertheless he kept remarkably cheerful although the visits to the workshop were less frequent. At that time the 14th century glass belonging to the Great West Window was stored in the Crypt. This noted glass had been releaded in 1930, so the Dean knew that the mediaeval glass would not need releading, although certain alterations to the glass would be required.

The severity of his illness prompted him to make certain arrangements concerning the future restoration of this most important window. He arranged that I should join him in the Crypt workshop at periodic intervals so that he could examine every panel. The panels were placed on an illuminated screen and from his seated position he indicated which pieces should be altered or removed. This was a noticeably tiring experience for him, yet he was pleased when after about five weeks his examination of the West Window glass had been completed. In the event this glass was not returned to its position in the Minster until 1967, four years after his death, but at least it went back with the alterations carried out as he would have wished.

The year 1962 was to be the Dean's last full year at the Minster, and it saw him organize and carry out his responsibilities at the Enthronement of Donald Coggan as Archbishop of York. As far as the stained glass was concerned, work was continuing on the windows of the Chapter House and Vestibule and also the Choir Clerestory. By now Mr. Nowland had retired and the small glazing team consisted of Mr. Lazenby and myself. In his letter to the Friends in the Annual Report for that year the Dean wrote:

'What are our glaziers to do when the reinsertion ends? The one unthinkable thing would be to break up the masterly combination of Lazenby and Gibson. Not only have they worked patiently through these huge fields of old glass, but in addition to their unique excellence as technicians, they have achieved knowledge no less unique not only in a rare artistic connoisseurship but in antiquarian scholarship. Gratitude, admiration and need alike bid the Minster keep the little team together; half their year's work will always be required to keep our 130 ancient windows in condition; and we are laying plans whereby any spare time can be devoted to ancient glass elsewhere. Already they have accepted and begun work on the great St Martin window for St Martin-le-Grand, on other parish churches in York, All Saints, North Street and St Martin-cum-Gregory. Outside York we have given assistance to a parish church and to the Cathedral in Carlisle and to old glass in Derbyshire.'

The 'plans' he referred to about working on glass elsewhere referred to the seeds that were being sown at that time by both Lord Kilmaine, Secretary of the Pilgrim Trust, and the Dean, which eventually emerged in 1967 in the formation of the York Glaziers' Trust – so, as always, the Dean was looking to the future.

As the months passed by the Dean became frailer and frailer as his illness took its toll and his days of visiting the workshop were over. I recall being with him shortly before he was confined to the Deanery. He was in a wheelchair and being led around the Minster on one of the final inspections by Mr. Jesse Green. The Dean invited me to accompany him into the Lady Chapel to look at the masterpiece of glass painting by John Thornton of Coventry in 1405–1408 as it was also the masterpiece of the Dean's creative restoration skills, 1944–1953. The Dean sat for fully five minutes in silence, looking upwards at the great wall of 15th century glass totally overcome, and then with tears in his eyes (which I know were of joy and not sadness) his weakened voice said 'that was a job well done'.

The next time I saw the Dean was only two days before he died, when he invited special friends to the Deanery to bid them farewell. Conversation by then was impossible – we held hands together silently as I knelt by his bedside and with a great effort he whispered to me, 'Always care for the Minster glass'.

REGRETS

First, I regret that Canon Frederick Harrison, Chancellor of York Minster, who died in 1958 and whose knowledge of the Minster glass was very considerable, was not brought more by the Dean into the discussions that took place about the re-ordering of the Minster glass. Harrison carried out a considerable study of the glass after coming to York in 1919 as a Vicar Choral, and was responsible for raising considerable funds towards the preservation of the windows in the 1920's and 1930's. His book on The *Painted Glass of York* (1927) is a valuable acquisition for all scholars in the field of stained glass. The Dean did invite the Chancellor into the workshop on occasions but I always felt that Harrison would dearly have loved to have been more fully involved in the work.

Secondly, the other person that I wish could have been brought more into the discussions concerning the re-ordering of the Minster glass was John Alder Knowles (d. 1961). His knowledge and scholarship of the art and craft of stained glass were hard to equal and, in particular, his knowledge of York glass which culminated in his *Essays on the York School of Glass Painting* (1936), was second to none, and yet this expertise was not used by the Dean as I thought would have been profitable for the Minster Glass.

I am fully aware as a junior member of the workshop at that time that there may well have been good reasons for not involving more fully these two distinguished scholars that it was not my place to know. All I will say is that it should never be forgotten that the continuing preservation of the stained glass of York Minster and the City of York owes much to the contribution they made both in scholarship and the well-being of the craft many years ago.

Let me now share a few personal memories about that great post-war restoration task.

CHURCH OF ST JOHN, MICKLEGATE

A stroke of good fortune for the Dean was that in 1944 the Dean and Chapter were given glass from the redundant York Church of St John, Micklegate, which was later to become the Arts Centre. Two windows containing 14th and 15th century glass in a disordered state could be used as the Dean and Chapter wished. It was this glass which provided the Dean with the perfect opportunity to exercise his creative skills whch he had used years earlier on the glass of King's College Chapel, Cambridge. It is worthy of comment that the Dean had great art-historical and iconographic knowledge of ancient glass, but this was allied also to technical skills. Indeed it was with much pride and contentment that he once showed me in King's College Chapel, Cam-

Plate 10.   The choir – south aisle. This crucifixion scene of French stained glass, *c.*1530, was originally in the church of St Jean in Rouen, and in the early part of the 19th century was installed in the East Window of St Mary's parish church, Rickmansworth. (Photograph: Peter Gibson, reproduced by permission of the Dean and Chapter of York.)

bridge, a tracery panel which he had glazed himself in one of the side Chapels. The Dean decided that the St John's glass should be installed after restoration in the windows of the West Wall of the K.O.Y.L.I. chapel. When in St John's Church, Micklegate, most of the ancient glass was in two windows namely:

SOUTH AISLE – EAST WINDOW

A window of three lights of 14th century glass depicting scenes from the life of St John the Baptist. This glass after re-ordering was installed in the two southernmost windows of the West wall of the K.O.Y.L.I. Chapel.

NORTH AISLE – EAST WINDOW

A four-light window containing late 15th century glass given to the church of Sir Richard Yorke (d. 1498) who was Lord Mayor of York in 1469 and 1482 and was also M.P. for the City. Some re-ordering of glass took place in the upper part of the two centre lights, with one panel which contained an assortment of mediaeval glass being identified by the Dean as representing a Corpus Christi procession. The tracery panels displayed angels holding shields and were remarkably well preserved. The Yorke window was inserted into the two northernmost windows of the West Wall of the K.O.Y.L.I. Chapel.

It was this glass that replaced the 19th century glass shaken out by the unexploded bomb which fell close to the Minster during the 1939–45 war and which the Dean referred to in his first letter to the Friends in their Annual Report of 1942. Medieval glass from other windows in St John's Church was also used by the Dean in the K.O.Y.L.I. Chapel, including two tracery panels depicting St George and St Michael which he used as the centre piece of the two central medallions in the northern lancet windows of the Chapel. A little surprising was the Dean's liberal use of modern glass above these figures, as he was always very careful in his mixing of ancient and modern glass.

EXCAVATED GLASS

Part of the halo of St George is made up of excavated glass from Watton Priory near Beverley. This historic site was once the largest house of the Order of Gilbert of Sempringham, founded in 1139. In 1946 Mr. Pexton, the owner of Watton Priory, during his excavations of the site, found many pieces of both coloured and white glass, which he gave to the Dean for use in the Minster windows. Much of the glass was heavily corroded and in need of meticulous cleaning, and the Dean

Plates 11 and 12. The choir – north aisle (easternmost window). This French glass of *c*.1600 depicts in seven scenes the legend of St James the Great; the top right-hand scene is a 19th-century nativity scene. The Dean obtained the panels for the Minster from Haseley Court, Oxfordshire and installed them in memory of his three brothers. One glass (above right) now constitutes a memorial to Dean Eric Milner-White. (Photographs: Peter Gibson, reproduced by permission of the Dean and Chapter of York.)

took it upon himself to spend hours carrying out the cleaning work both in the Deanery and also on his rail journeys, much to the mystification of his fellow travellers.

I remember on one occasion he was travelling to London to attend Convocation at Church House and he took with him about two dozen pieces of the Watton glass that was so blackened that it was impossible to see any colour or detail of the glass. On his return to York and the workshop at the end of the week he triumphantly placed the thoroughly cleaned pieces of Watton glass on the bench and said with more than a degree of pride: *That* is what I have achieved at Convocation!' Some of these pieces were glazed together to make a small panel which can be seen at the top of the central light of the second window from the east in the South Aisle of the Nave.

ST STEPHEN'S CHAPEL
EAST WINDOW

The first Minster window to be replaced after the 1939–45 War was one which I think is one of the most under-appreciated windows in the Cathedral – the East window of St Stephen's Chapel. The lovely blend of red, white and blue glass, combined with the delicate use of silver stain which was used to such stunning effect by the 15th century glass painters, is seen to great advantage in this window. Admittedly the 14th century figure of St James in the central light breaks up the unity of the window but, notwithstanding, this is one of the finest windows in the Cathedral. Especially noteworthy are the angels with their musical instruments in the tracery.

Modest re-ordering of the glass in the main lights was carried out but the top tracery panel presented a real challenge – it was truly a jigsaw of ancient glass. There was sufficient original glass visible to indicate that the panel was meant to portray the Virgin and Child with attendant angels around. The suckling Christ-child was clearly visible but where the head of the Virgin should have been was a splendid Royal Shield of King Henry VIII. The lower half of the Virgin's garment was missing and instead a large piece of chequered flooring had been inserted together with a small roundel bordered by rays of glory.

Immense care and thought went into the reconstruction of this panel and, even though it was one of the earliest re-arrangement tasks carried out by the Dean, I believe it was one of the most successful. It certainly set a standard of excellence for future projects.

Plates 13 and 14. The reconstruction of the virgin and child in the top panel of the East Window of St Stephen's chapel (before, above, and after, right) was one of Dean Milner-White's earliest rearrangements of Minster glass. (Photographs reproduced by permission of the Dean and Chapter of York.)

THE ZOUCHE CHAPEL

This lovely Chapel off the South Choir Aisle of the Minster was the Dean's favourite Chapel, although it was closely rivalled by All Saints at the east end of the aisle.

It was in the south wall windows of the chapel that the Dean decided to house the many birds and animals and pieces of particular interest that were located in misplaced positions in many of the Minster windows. The reason for this decision was that the windows contained plain quarry (diamond-shaped) glazing and that the ferramenta conveniently divided the windows openings into the required spaces to frame the pieces of glass.

Hunting for these pieces among the hundreds of Minster panels in storage during the post-war period was one of the most exciting and educational periods of my apprenticeship. At that time many panels were stored in the Crypt, and the Dean arranged that a bench and an illuminated display screen should be installed there, enabling examination and work on the panels to take place. Many of the fascinating pieces now in the south wall windows of the Chapel were located in these panels. One great disappointment to the Dean was that he was unable to locate a dancer with ribbons which was illustrated in the account of the *Stained and Painted Glass of York* by George Benson. If future restorers of the Minster glass ever find this piece then I hope room will be found for it in the Zouche Chapel windows. However the sheer enjoyment the Dean and I had in searching through the panels was endless and probably the greatest thrill was the finding of the famous Wren and the Spider. This is a very fragile piece of mediaeval glass and I was very apprehensive indeed when the Dean entrusted me with the task of taking it out of its misplaced position. The actual release of the piece took about two hours of careful cutting of the lead and solder which encased the glass. The Dean, once having given the order to take the piece out, left me to the task, saying he would come back in two hours; this he did, and there was a minor celebration when he returned and saw the piece safe and sound on the bench. I do wish many more people could have seen the Dean during these working sessions and have witnessed his almost schoolboy-like enthusiasm when particular pieces were found.

THE EAST WINDOW OF THE ZOUCHE CHAPEL

Until the Dean's purchase of the three figures of the Bishop, King and Cardinal to be seen in the lower of the East window of the Chapel, the total window was a kaleidoscope of coloured mediaeval glass. It is believed that much of the glass was surviving pieces from the De

Mauley windows in the South Nave Aisle, which was ill restored outside York at the beginning of this century.

The medley of glass in the East window developed into being a 'bank' of glass which the Dean drew on quite liberally during the post-war period. Time and time again I would go over to the Chapel with him and he would select certain pieces for removal to assist in the glazing of particular panels in the workshop.

THE CREATION OF A 'NEW' NAVE WINDOW

From about the middle of the 17th century until 1952 the western most window of the South Nave Aisle contained plain quarry (dia-mond-shaped) glazing – the mediaeval stained glass having vanished. When the Dean in 1950 discovered some panels of 14th century glass misplaced in various windows in the Minster he decided he would use them to 'create' a new Nave window. The panels that he found were both figurative and canopies (architectural details) and were ideally suited for re-deployment in the Nave. The Dean considered it essential that the repetitive design of the 14th century windows of the Nave aisles, namely a double tier of both canopy and figure panels alternating with grisaille, should be retained. The panels to be used in the new window were found in the Chapter House Windows, the St Cuthbert window in the South Choir Aisle and also a North Choir Aisle window.

The figurative panels consisted of figures of Saints: St Lawrence, St Stephen, St Cuthbert, St Peter and St John the Evangelist. However, at the final count of the required six-figure and six-canopy panels the Dean was one short of each. There were also available for use three later 14th century figure panels depicting the Annunciation to the Shepherds, the Meeting of Joachim and Anna at the Golden Gate, and the Annuniciation to the Blessed Virgin Mary. Some criticism of the use of these three panels in this window was expressed when he placed them in the three lower positions of the central light, thereby disrupting the repetitive design of the other Nave windows (with the exception of the Jesse window). Further criticism also followed when a panel was made up from fragments depicting the Purification and installed in the lower left-hand panel of the window.

The Dean, I am sure, was perceptive enough to foresee the criticism that his new window would receive – all I will say is that the 'creation' of this window was a truly remarkable achievement. At the present time (1991) the Dean and Chapter are planning to transfer the Purification scene to a North Nave Aisle window.

Plates 15 and 16. The upper section of the Nave Jesse window (*c.*1310) before and after restoration. (Photographs reproduced by permission of the Dean and Chapter of York.)

THE FALL OF MAN

It was in 1947 that the Dean purchased from the owner of Potternewton House in Leeds some exceptionally fine 16th century panels of the Rouen School of glass painting. These panels, depicting the Fall of Man, found their way to England – as much continental glass did – after the French Revolutionary wars.

The Dean placed these panels first in the easternmost window of the North Choir Aisle, and later transferred them to their present position above the 17th century Salutation scene in All Saints Chapel. These panels were among the first in the Minster to receive the new external protective glazing which mainly matched the contours and designs of the ancient glass.

A TREE OF JESSE RESTORED

The re-ordering of this window – the third from East in the South Aisle of the Nave was, apart from the restoration of the East window, the Dean's finest work in the Minster. The 14th century glass had become totally misordered with the passing of the centuries, and with the leadwork also badly deteriorated it was an ideal candidate for the attention of the Dean.

The Dean took the photographs of each panel away with him when he went on holiday in 1950. On the day of his return he rushed into the workshop waving the photographs above his head and shouting excitedly 'It's here – the Jesse window is here!' He had spent his entire holiday sorting through the photographic record and making notes on the creation of the missing figures, the re-ordering of the missing background glass, and, most importantly, the realigning of the stem of the Tree, which is a vital feature in windows of this subject depicting the ancestry of Christ. One particular panel which caused difficulty was the lower central panel, which depicted the figure of Jesse. The figure was completely missing and so the Dean called in Harry Stammers, the glass painter based at nearby Gray's Court, to assist in the drawing of the figure. Even Stammers was a little uncertain as to the actual posture of the figure, so the Dean asked me to act as a 'model'. I had to lie on the workshop bench in a variety of postures until in their joint opinion the right position was found, and then Stammers transferred the necessary outlines onto paper and so the figure of Jesse was created!

This was the first Nave window in the Minster to receive new external protective glazing shaped and leaded to the same design as the medieval glass. The restoration of this window was therefore both an art-historical and technical triumph for the Dean.

CONTROVERSIAL REDEPLOYMENT OF PANELS

In 1960/61 the Dean decided that some figurative panels of 14th century glass from the Nave Clerestory should be re-positioned in the lower panels of the windows in the East wall of the South Transept and below the 18th century Peckitt figures in the South wall. At the same time he placed three of the displaced 18th century panels (albeit temporarily) at the bottom of the three central lights above the Five Sisters Window in the North Transept. His argument for the re-siting of the panels in the South Transept was that he considered that the panels were of exceptional interest and should be seen at close quarters – a view not supported by everyone.

It should be placed on record that all these nine panels in the South Transept have subsequently been replaced in their original position in the Nave Clerestory and the three Peckitt panels also reinstated in their original position.

ST VINCENT

One of the most remarkable figures created by the Dean was the 14th century figure of St Vincent in the central light of the fourth window from the East in the North Choir Aisle.

When the time came to re-insert this glass in 1958 it was realized that the glass in the central light was so badly corroded that it could not be replaced. Providentially some pieces of 14th century glass found in a Minster storeroom were obviously part of a figure. There was other glass of the same date in the bank of glass held in the glaziers workshop, and so the Dean decided to create a mediaeval figure holding a book and a short knife. Some Lombardic lettering was found of 14th century date (earlier than the figure, in my opinion), and from this glass he arranged the letters to identify the figure as St Bartholomew. A close friend of the Dean later identified the created figure as St Vincent, the Spanish deacon, but the lettering proclaiming the first identification of the figure still stands in the window.

THE DEAN'S GREATEST ACHIEVEMENT
THE GREAT EAST WINDOW

Without doubt the masterpiece of the Dean's creative abilities as far as the post-war restoration of the Minster glass was concerned was his work on the Great East Window. This incomparable window, which was painted between 1405 and 1408 by John Thornton of Coventry and his team of craftsmen, is 76 feet in height and 32 feet in width. There are 161 tracery panels and in the nine lights below 117 square panels, each of the latter being approximately three feet square. The tracery

Plates 17 and 18.   The Great East Window (1405–1408). Noah's Ark before and after restoration. (Photographs reproduced by permission of the Dean and Chapter of York.)

panels display a vast Heavenly Host of Archangels, Angels, Kings, Prophets and Saints, and at the summit of the window in the top tracery panel is the figure of God the Father with an open book bearing the words Alpha and Omega, which is the theme of the window. The beginning can be seen in the first three rows of panels above the upper gallery, which recount in 27 Old Testament scenes the events from the Creation to the Death of Absalom. Below the gallery are nine rows containing 81 panels illustrating the end – the last book of the Bible, the Revelation of St John the Divine. The lowest row displays legendary and historical figures linked with Christianity in the North of England and the See of York, both noted ecclesiastics and kings, with the central panel showing the figure of Walter Skirlaw, Bishop of Durham (1388–1406), the donor of this great window, which is generally regarded as being the finest 15th century stained glass window in the world.

THE 1829 FIRE

It is known that major work took place on the glass only three years before the Minster fire of 1829. How the window escaped serious damage is difficult to understand. Having handled every single panel of glass in the window I can say without hesitation that there were no traces of fire-cracked glass in any of the panels. However there were many instances where 19th century glass had been inserted in the panels as a means of effecting temporary repair, possibly after the fire.

The releading of the tracery panels under the Dean's supervision began in 1944 after he had requested that a small number of panels should be brought from their war-time storage location to the workshop. The leadwork of the panels was very buckled, and much of the glass was covered with deposits of what I believe were the remains of soot particles due to the fire. It was necessary to flatten the panels by immersing them in water in a lead-lined tank which still survives in the workshop.

The releading of the tracery panels, followed by the Old Testament scenes, gained momentum after the war, and the Dean's supervision of the restoration work saw him visiting the workshop two or three times a day. His policy where pieces of glass were missing was to utilise if possible pieces of similar date and design that were available in the bank of glass in the workshop. He was however quite prepared to use 14th century glass which was thought to have originally been in North Choir Clerestory windows, and also 19th century glass from the window itself, as a last resort if no 15th century glass was available.

Little glass was discarded throughout the restoration of the East Window, the Dean insisting that as much as possible of the glass that came out of the window should be re-used. This policy was especially emphasized with the re-ordering of the Old Testament scene illustrating Noah's Ark – none of the 15th century Ark remained and so the Dean used 14th century canopy glass (architectural details) to create a 'new' Ark. Likewise the panel showing Samson pulling down the pillars of the Temple was re-ordered using 14th century glass to advantage.

The Old Testament scenes presented the greatest challenge as some were the most seriously disordered panels, and it is not an exaggeration to say that not one single piece of inserted glass went into those particular panels unless it was approved by the Dean. As work progressed on to the Revelation panels there was not so much misordered glass as had been encountered in the early part of the work on the window. The Dean's enthusiasm for the work on this window never wavered, and one felt sometimes that he was almost disappointed when panels were found to be in a reasonably well-ordered state and not demanding his specialized skills.

He did have five favourite panels in the Revelation series – not because of the problems they caused, but simply because of the composition of the panels. These were:

    The Altar with Seven Candlesticks
    The Seven Churches of Asia
    St John setting sail for Patmos
    The Four Winds
    The Dragon giving power to the Beast with seven heads.

No fewer than 30 panels in the East window – five Old Testament scenes and 25 in the Revelation series – were found to be in the wrong order and were re-ordered into their correct sequence.

The Dean's own account of the work on this window is in the Annual Reports of the Friends of York Minster and should ideally be read when one is viewing the glass. However his words will never truly convey his own dedication and single-mindedness in directing this great restoration task from beginning to end and bringing it to a triumphant conclusion for which posterity will be ever grateful.

THE CHAPTER HOUSE
THE EAST WINDOW

The most controversial restoration of stained glass carried out by the Dean in the Minster concerned the re-arrangement of glass in the East window of the Chapter House. The seven large windows in the Chapter House are approximately fifty feet in height and twenty feet in width. Six windows contain glass of c 1300 displayed in four rows of figurative panels alternating with grisaille. Heraldic glass features in the tracery panels, some of which had been restored by William Peckitt of York in the 18th century.

However, the seventh window (which was the East window) had been restored in 1845 by John Barnett of York (1786–1859), who painted copies of the mediaeval glass, both the figurative scenes and the grisaille. One original panel depicting the Ascension had survived this restoration in the central position of the lowest row of figurative scenes. It is still a mystery why the mediaeval glass in this window had deteriorated so badly by the middle of the 19th century that it had to be replaced by a modern copy. The surviving panel of the Ascension scene certainly contained weathered glass but was in no worse condition than the mediaeval glass in other Chapter House windows.

The tracery panels of the Chapter House windows were not removed for safety during the 1939–1945 war – a policy which also applied to tracery sections of the Choir Clerestory windows.

The Dean decided in 1959 that the Barnett 'copies' should be replaced by other glass which he considered more appropriate to its setting in the Chapter House. For this purpose he had to gather a total of 44 panels, which he did from a variety of locations in Minster windows. These locations were the Nave Clerestory (panels of 15th century glass illustrating the Life of Christ, and five panels of 16th century glass), the easternmost window of the North Choir Aisle (two panels of 16th century glass) and the second window from the East in the North Nave Aisle (two panels of 16th century glass). All the 16th century figurative panels depicted scenes from the life of Thomas Becket.

The Dean's redeployment of these panels in the East window was as follows:

The ten 15th century scenes he used for the top two rows of figurative panels. The nine 16th century panels he used for the two lowest rows of figurative panels, the tenth panel being the surviving 14th century panel.

A major problem, however, still remained, as he needed 25 grisaille panels, and his solution of this problem was the most controversial part of the project. He utilised the 25 grisaille panels from the South West window of the Chapter House (excluding the borders). His justifiction for this drastic action was that he considered that the grisaille glass in its original setting in the South West window was never seen to advantage because of the shadow cast on the window by the Eastern side of the North Transept and the Central Tower. The Dean now had sufficient panels to make the 'new' window, the last part of the jigsaw being the retention in the East window of the Barnett borders.

One remaining problem was that he still had to find glass for the spaces vacated in the South West window of the Chapter House by the removal of the grisaille panels. He decided to make these panels from mediaeval glass in storage in the bank of glass held in the workshop, supplemented by modern tinted antique glass and some of the lighter pieces of 19th century grisaille glass from the East window.

The East window therefore now contains four different periods of glass painting, and the South West window has 25 'new' grisaille panels. It will be seen, therefore, why the restoration of the East window is still being judged as a controversial restoration.

THE BECKET PANELS

The nine panels of 16th century glass illustrating the life of Thomas Becket are part of a series of at least thirteen panels known to exist. The remaining four panels are to be seen in a North wall window of the nearby Parish Church of St Michael le Belfrey. From pieces of glass that I have seen in misplaced positions in other Minster windows there were undoubtedly additional panels to this series. The Dean's theory about the Becket panels was that they originated in the former parish church of St Wilfrid's which stood in Blake Street York, and which was demolished in 1585, when the parish was united with that of St Michael le Belfrey. At some time since then these 16th century panels were divided for use between their present two locations.

Postscript Towards the end of 1961 the Dean entered the Purey-Cust Nursing Home for an operation. He asked if I would drop him a note from time to time informing him of progress in the workshop. At that time repairs were taking place at my home in Precentor's Court overlooking the Nursing Home, and I said in one of my letters that I was using a rubber hammer so as not to cause him any sleeplessness.

THE DEANERY, YORK
Telephone: 23608
4 December 1961

My dear MAN from the Glass Shop,

No longer *LAD*; no longer *Apprentice*; something of a *Neighbour* still, even if a little bit further off!

First, let me thank you for your kindly wishes, even if they were only remembered at the end in a P.S. Secondly, for your long letter; thirdly, for the blisters and cuts which you still suffer daily on behalf of the Minster, not to speak of the beads of perspiration, which seem, however, reduced to the moment when you are waiting for the weekly packet; and last, but not least, for the noble gift of chrysanthemums.

It is true that while at the Home I was greatly disturbed by lusty hammerings, but they were not such as could have been delivered by a rubber hammer, and so I can absolve you from your fears, and indeed thank you for your thoughtfulness!

You need not fear that the Master Glazier will yet appear to renew your quiverings, as wounds will not be healed for some five weeks, although he will do his best to get to church on Christmas Day in the hopes of seeing the ex-apprentice still working in his limited time.

Do give my affectionate regards to Lazenby, and my good wishes for his health. You can tell him that the Pilgrim Trust are giving us a sum of £700 to finish things off next year. Presently I shall be glad to hear how the St Martin's glass and ours are getting on. The Master Glazier will be delighted to mount the steps and inspect the benches once again!

Ever yours gratefully,
Eric Milner-White

Index